THE FlyPast BOOK OF THE

B-17
FLYING FORTRESS

ROBERT J. RUDHALL

KEY
BOOKS

Above: Teamwork was vital when operating a Flying Fortress during combat. Here, aircrew and groundcrew of B-17G *Thundermug* gather for a 'group shot' in front of their aircraft. (US National Archives)

Below: Probably posed especially for the cameras, this B-17F's crew check out the mission's route one last time, before boarding the bomber and heading off to the 'target for today'. (US National Archives)

Key Books Ltd
PO Box 100, Stamford, Lincolnshire PE9 1XQ
United Kingdom

Telephone: +44 (0) 1780 755131
E-mail: keybooks@keypublishing.com

First published in Great Britain by Key Books Ltd
in 2002

ISBN 0-946219-59-1

British Library Cataloguing in Publication Data:
A catalogue record for this book is available from the
British Library

Designed by DAG Publications Ltd
Printed in Spain by Book Print

The classic shape of the
Boeing B-17G Flying
Fortress *Yankee Lady*. Its
highly polished skin reflects
the bright Texas sunshine.
(KEY – Duncan Cubitt)

CONTENTS

① THE HISTORY

BOEING B-17 Flying Fortress, the name alone was a great morale booster for the Americans during World War Two. The aircraft served valiantly on many fronts, and although in production numbers was outstripped by Consolidated's B-24 Liberator, it is the B-17 which somehow sums up the USA's spirit of freedom in those dark days.

Its genesis can be traced back to Boeing's Model 294, a four-engined giant of a machine, which was designed to meet an Army Air Corps (AAC) requirement, issued on April 14, 1934. Its designation was changed to XB-15 in July 1936, but by then the project was overtaken by the company's next bomber on the drawing board, the Model 299. The 299 had been designed and built in an incredibly short space of time, at Boeing's own expense, to qualify for inclusion in the AAC's competition at Wright Field in August 1935. Initial work on the new aircraft began on June 18, 1934, with construction starting on August 16. Progress on the project was, to say the least, rapid and the prototype took to the air for the first time from Boeing Field, Seattle, on July 28, 1935. Earlier that month the aircraft had been revealed to the press and public. A reporter for the *Seattle Times* used the term '15-Ton Flying Fortress' in his coverage of the auspicious event. That was it. The name struck a chord with Boeing executives and within a matter of days 'Flying Fortress' was registered as a company name for the Model 299.

Incorporating design and construction aspects from the successful twin-engined Boeing 247 and the unfinished XB-15, a number of test flights were carried out on the 299 before it embarked on a marathon flight (for a prototype aircraft) to Wright Field for evaluation. It flew the 2,000 miles (3,218km) at an average speed of 252mph (405km/h). It therefore emerged as a clear winner over the other bomber types on test, but tragically was lost in an accident on October 30, when it took off with the flying controls in the locked position. All five crew on board were killed.

Even though the aircraft's full military capability had not been explored in detail, enough of the AAC 'top brass' were sufficiently impressed to place a service test order for 13 examples of the Model 299. It was then given the military designation of B-17, it being the 17th bomber type to be operated by the AAC. Building a new factory, known as Plant 2, Boeing commenced work on the service test YB-17s. By August 1937, all 13 had been delivered and the majority of these were assigned to the 2nd Bombardment Group (BG) at Langley Field, Virginia. A 14th machine, originally intended to be a static test airframe, was fitted with turbo-supercharged engines and flown on experimental tests. The results were impressive to say the least and it was obvious that the supercharged engine was the way forward and would become a standard 'fit' to all B-17s manufactured in the future.

Despite those pilots and crews who flew the aircraft being impressed with what they saw, orders for the new bomber were slow to be placed. It was during this period that the B-17s made a number of long-distance goodwill flights across Central and South America, setting a number of records in the process. These exercises gained the type widespread publicity and the name Flying Fortress became a household word with the press and public alike! Even during this hiatus, Boeing was working on improvements to the basic B-17 airframe. It was not until war clouds were gathering in Europe, around the time of the Munich Crisis, that AAC chiefs were able to secure an

Right: With the sun glinting off the rear fuselage, the XB-15 is escorted by another Boeing product, the diminutive P-26 Peashooter. (Key Collection)

Below The giant Boeing Model 294 was subsequently re-designated as the XB-15 in 1936. Nicknamed *Old Grandpappy*, it was then the largest aircraft of its type in the world, with a staggering 139ft (42.3m) wingspan, which incorporated an internal passageway running from the fuselage cabin to the engines. This permitted inspection, and sometimes repairs, to be carried out while the aircraft was in flight. On July 30, 1939, the XB-15 broke the world record for weight lifting, previously held by the Russian-built *Maxim Gorky*. (Key Collection)

Above: In 1938, Boeing Y1B-17A 36-149 was initially assigned to the 4000th Army Air Force Base Unit and was based at Wright Field, Ohio. (Robert F Dorr)

increase in defence spending from the politicians. The first B-17Bs entered military service in late 1939 and by the following year contracts for 250 aircraft had been placed, with a further order for the improved B-17C. With more powerful Wright Cyclone engines and heavier armament, the B-17C was the first of the classic B-17 variants.

It was the B-17C that was the first variant of the bomber to go to war. Flown to the UK, under the Lend-Lease agreement, they were delivered to the Royal Air Force (RAF) as Fortress Is. After flying the Atlantic, the 20 aircraft were modified at Burtonwood to meet the RAF's requirements, and were then flown on high altitude operations with 90 Squadron, 2 Group RAF Bomber Command, based initially at Watton. The unit subsequently transferred to West Raynham when the all-grass airfield at Watton was found to be unsuitable for heavy four-

Right: Safely positioned behind guide ropes, the prototype Flying Fortress awaits the press at Seattle on July 17, 1935. For its day the aircraft was a revelation in design and construction. Built with no firm contract from the US Government, this large commitment from the then relatively medium-sized Boeing company was indeed a high-risk venture. (Robert F Dorr)

Below: This YB-17 served with the 2nd Bomb Group during 1938 and was based at Langley Field. (Pete West)

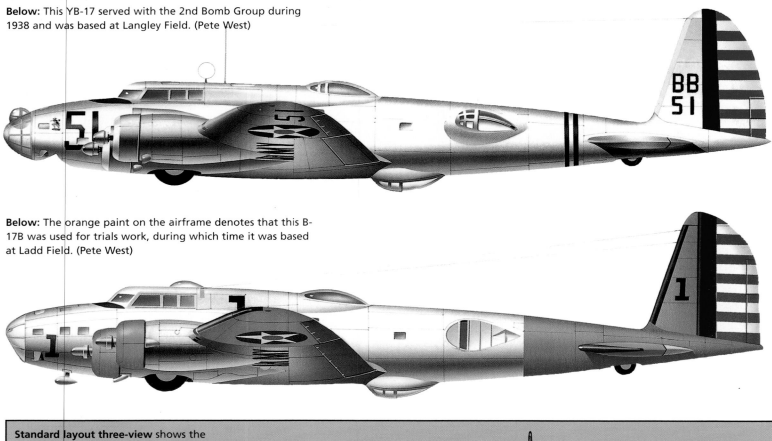

Below: The orange paint on the airframe denotes that this B-17B was used for trials work, during which time it was based at Ladd Field. (Pete West)

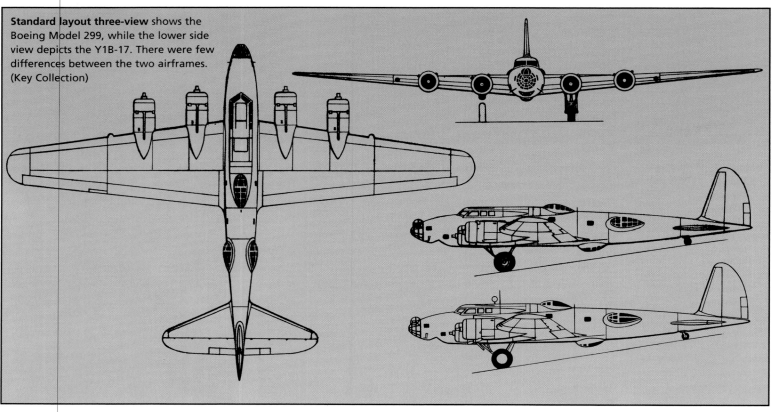

Standard layout three-view shows the Boeing Model 299, while the lower side view depicts the Y1B-17. There were few differences between the two airframes. (Key Collection)

Left: Several experimental camouflage schemes were applied to the early model B-17s. Some of them were quite garish and totally impractical. Y1B-17 36-152, then serving with the 20th Bomb Squadron, forsook its natural metal finish during the GHQ Air Force anti-aircraft manoeuvres during May 1938. (Key Collection)

Below: Flying Fortress I 40-2066 (AN530) 'WP-F' was also one of those that flew on the early operations of the type with 90 Squadron RAF. It lasted until September 1943, when it was struck off charge. (Pete West)

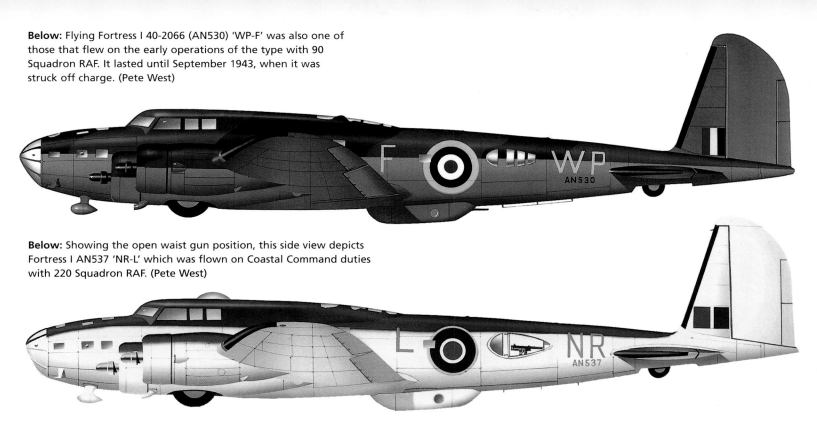

Below: Showing the open waist gun position, this side view depicts Fortress I AN537 'NR-L' which was flown on Coastal Command duties with 220 Squadron RAF. (Pete West)

Below: The B-17C/D models were the first real mass production variants. Modifications included the installation of engine superchargers, a redesigned nose, modified and enlarged waist and under-fuselage gun positions and the addition of an aircraft commander's Plexiglas bubble behind the pilots. (Robert F Dorr)

engined aircraft. These operations were not a success, showing up a number of weaknesses in the B-17's systems. At heights of 20,000ft (6,096m) windows frosted over making visibility difficult and the on-board oxygen equipment was prone to freezing, leading to complete failure. Turbo-superchargers became sensitive in their operation as altitude was gained, requiring careful handling.

Internal communication was made almost impossible due to microphones and switches also freezing up. Externally, the engines were prone to blowing oil out of the rocker cover breathers, which if prolonged could threaten the integrity of both the engine and airframe. Despite these difficulties, the Fortress Is were often operated at heights of 35,000ft (10,668m), putting considerable strain on their crews and the machines.

More improvements were on the way, with the B-17E, which incorporated significant airframe and armament changes. The B-17E first flew in September 1941 and although its performance was slightly poorer than the previous models, it did handle better at high altitudes. After the Japanese attack on Pearl Harbor Hawaii, on December 7, 1941, the need for B-17s was paramount. However, the parent company was not in a position to vastly increase its output, so the prospects of licence-building the bomber came under scrutiny with Douglas

and Lockheed-Vega deemed to be those offering the most suitable facilities. Corresponding with these new production arrangements came yet another upgrade in the shape of the B-17F, which became the first standard production variant for all three factories.

More powerful engines, extra fuel capacity and, depending on the bomb load, an increase in range, were all attributes boasted by the B-17F. When the US 8th Air Force (AF) arrived in the UK during the summer of 1942, it was B-17Es and B-17Fs that the flying units brought with them. Even though the crews had undergone intensive training in the USA, it soon became obvious that familiarisation with the theatre in which they would be operating would be urgently needed before any serious efforts could be made to take the war back to Germany. At that time, the RAF was giving out warnings to the 8th AF's High Command about the dangers of flying long-range, unescorted daylight raids over enemy-occupied territory. This was based on bitter experience gained during 1940 and 1941. These warnings were largely ignored and 8th AF B-17 operations commenced with an attack on Rouen, France, on August 17, 1942. This was accomplished without loss to the attacking force, thus giving a misleading impression of what European bombing raids could entail.

Above: The Flying Fortress's first American baptism of fire took place at Pearl Harbor, Hawaii, on December 7, 1941, when six B-17Cs and eight B-17Es of the 7th and 19th Bomb Groups arrived over the islands in the midst of the Japanese attack. Five B-17C/Ds, which were being used for island defence, were destroyed on the ground at Hickham Field, with several others being badly damaged. (Robert F Dorr)

Left: B-17C 40-2068 (AN531) was one of 20 Fortress Is, purchased by the RAF from United States Army Air Corps stocks, which were delivered 'across the pond' between May and July 1941. These early marks of B-17 were not successful within the RAF due to them being employed on high-level missions which were not suited to the aircraft. This aircraft served with 90 and 220 Squadrons, as well as spending some time with the Royal Aircraft Establishment at Boscombe Down, where this photograph was taken in 1944. It was struck off charge on January 17, 1945. (Key Collection)

Right: Repair and modification centres were also kept busy during wartime. In this view, B-17Gs receive copious attention before being re-issued to operational units. (US National Archives)

As the war progressed, in a co-ordinated effort between the British and American forces, the RAF bombed by night and the 8th AF bombed by day. In spite of the B-17's strong defensive armament, losses were starting to build up. On October 21, a force of 66 B-17s and 24 B-24s was sent to attack the U-boat pens at Lorient. This was the first real shock to the system for the UK-based commanders and aircraft crews. Bad weather over the target meant that only aircraft of the 97th Bomb Group (BG) actually carried out an attack. Three of its aircraft were lost to enemy fighters. Another six sustained damage. In sheer percentage terms the raid was an unmitigated disaster. This 20 per cent loss rate, if allowed to continue, would cripple the bomber force in a matter of weeks. It was obviously a major problem for which a solution had to be found.

Day after day mass formations of Fortresses (not forgetting the B-24s) and their crews fought their way to and from the enemy targets and engaged in some of the bloodiest aerial battles ever to take place in World War Two. Often operating in tight formations and relying on the sheer concentration of the defensive armament to ward off attacking Luftwaffe fighters, there were some horrendous losses, both in men and machines.

'In the field' armament modifications were carried out on the B-17s, with the addition of extra guns in the air-

craft's nose in order to combat the enemy's effective head-on attack tactics. This fundamental problem would not really be addressed until the B-17G, with its chin turret in the nose, came on-stream in 1943. By then, the 8th AF was sending escort fighters, P-38s, P-47s and the ultimate long-range escort fighter, the P-51, to help combat the German fighter force's increasing and effective interceptions of the mass bomber formations.

The B-17G was the final major mark of Boeing's famous bomber, with 4,025 built by Boeing, 2,395 by Douglas and 2,250 by Lockheed-Vega. The only external differences from the earlier models were the chin turret, staggered positions for the rear fuselage and nose gun operators. As from January 1944, B-17Gs were issued from the factories in natural metal finish, the need for camouflage paint being deemed to be unnecessary by that stage of the war. Some 85 B-17Gs were transferred to the RAF, operating under the Fortress III designation. These were operated within 100 Group and were flown on Radio Counter Measures duties.

While the Flying Fortress's use in the European war has always had the most coverage, the B-17 also served valiantly in the Pacific Theatre. This started with a veritable baptism of fire at Pearl Harbor on December 7, 1941, when a flight of six B-17Cs and eight B-17Es, en route to the Philippines, intended to make a stop-over at Hawaii.

Above: Later marks of Fortresses employed by the RAF were more successful in the roles with which they were tasked. This Fortress II, FK209 (which still wears its USAAC tail number) was one of 30 of the breed taken on charge by the RAF between April and July 1942. Employed on Coastal Command duties (note the aerials on the nose and underwing positions), it went missing during a patrol on March 23, 1943. (Key Collection)

Below right: During World War Two the Boeing, Douglas and Lockheed-Vega factories produced almost 13,000 B-17s of all variants. To quote President Roosevelt's famous words, the 'arsenal of democracy' worked overtime to provide the tools of war. Here, inner wing sections stretch as far as the eye can see. (US National Archives)

Arriving overhead at the same time as the Japanese attack, the unarmed Fortresses found themselves in the 'thick of it' and had to rapidly divert to other airfields. One even made an emergency landing on a nearby golf course!

In August 1942, a force of 15 B-17s began an assault on the Japanese stronghold at Rabaul. One crashed on take-off and two subsequently aborted with mechanical problems, the remaining dozen being intercepted by a force of Japanese Zero fighters above the target. While eleven of the Fortresses found safety in cloud cover, the other was shot down. In other areas, a number of B-17s were operated by the 25th Bomb Squadron on anti-submarine flights to guard the Panama Canal, while others were flown in the search and rescue role in the latter part of the war against Japan.

When World War Two came to an abrupt but thankful, end, with the dropping of two atomic bombs on Hiroshima and Nagasaki in Japan, B-17s were still pouring out from the production lines in the USA. In the immediate post-war years there would be little use for the B-17 in a civilian passenger transport role. The storage yards spread across the USA were full to the brim with former military aircraft waiting for buyers or the smelter. The average asking price for a Fortress at this time is reported to have been in the region of $13,000, although examples were sometimes sold for a lot less. By December 1945, unwanted bombers, fighters and the like were, on average, arriving at the rate of one per minute, often straight from the factory.

Some B-17s with confirmed operational records were lucky survivors, for example the famed *Memphis Belle,* 41-24485, was found in 1946 by a resident of Memphis, Tennessee, languishing at the Reconstruction Finance Corporation's (RFC) storage facility at Altus, Oklahoma. The bomber's identity was soon confirmed and arrangements were made by civic leaders of the city to have the aircraft transferred as a war memorial. Sadly, in ensuing years the Fortress suffered from the effects of the weather and vandals.

Several aborted attempts were made to restore the B-17 to its former glory, all of which resulted in the airframe failing to get the attention it deserved. Subsequent pressure by the US Air Force Museum saw a regularised organisation put in control of the *Memphis Belle's* future and the aircraft, now resident at Mud Island, is currently looking a lot healthier in the hands of the *Memphis Belle* Memorial Association.

From the thousands of war-surplus machines available, the B-17's size and multi-engined capability made it a suitable platform for the fire-fighting air tanker and sprayer role. Some 23 aircraft were converted and used for this purpose, starting in the early 1960s. Able to carry 2,000 gallons of fire retardant, two major organisations, Aero Union, based at Chico, California, and Aviation Specialities of Mesa, Arizona, gave the Fortress a new lease of life.

It was this role that was to eventually provide a number of airframes to the up-and-coming preservation

'industry'. When the B-17 came to the end of its useful life as a 'tanker' (due to shortages of spare parts during the late 1970s) several were traded with museums and individuals to help kick-start the warbird preservation movement which is so strong today.

The Fortress also saw limited use as a spraying aircraft, the major operator in this role being Dothan Aviation in Alabama. After being used to combat anything from infestations of budworms to the eradication of moths,

Flying Fortresses were retired from this occupation in the mid-1970s.

Throughout the famous design's operational career, it always gained the lion's share of publicity, over its Consolidated B-24 cousin, which for obvious reasons has always irked the Liberator crews. However, it was obvious that when the American publicity machine got hold of the well-proportioned, sleek-looking B-17 it would be milked for all the propaganda value it could sustain.

Above: During the mid-war years production of B-17s reached an all-time high with new aircraft rolling off of the production line at an amazing rate. Here, new B-17Gs are towed out from the factory for flight testing. (Boeing)

Left: A quartet of B-17Gs wearing the 'VE' codes of the 532nd Bomb Squadron, 381st Bomb Group, US 8th Air Force, head out from the UK to enemy-occupied Europe during the latter part of World War Two. (US National Archives)

Above right: Some B-17s came to grief before they reached the European Theatre of Operations (ETO). En route from the USA to the UK this B-17E force landed in the snow in Greenland. (FlyPast Collection)

Right: With its attendant groundcrew watching, B-17F *Idiots Delight* of the 94th Bomb Group starts its outer engines before embarking on its 50th operational mission, a trip to Berlin on March 22, 1944. (US National Archives)

Right: Four-engined bombers seldom saw the inside of a hangar during wartime. Routine maintenance took place outside and even major repairs, as this view illustrates, were sometimes carried out in the open air. (US National Archives)

Below: Returning from a mission, B-17G 43-37613 of the 324th Bomb Squadron, 91st Bomb Group, suffered an undercarriage collapse on landing. Despite the front chin turret being crushed and the bending of all four propellers, the airframe seems to have little other damage. (Robert F Dorr)

As a result, a number of wartime-produced films featured Boeing's B-17, usually in morale-boosting roles. The 'Fort' first appeared on screen as early as 1938 in MGM's *Test Pilot*, which featured Clark Gable. B-17s were also prominent in the 1943 Warner Bros production *Air Force*, which starred John Garfield, Gig Young and Charles Drake. But by far its most famous wartime appearance has to be William Wyler's *Memphis Belle*, released in 1944. Using colour film, itself something of a rarity during World War Two, it told the story of an 8th Air Force B-17 that survived to complete 25 missions. Following the actual aircraft and crew on their final raid in the European Theatre of Operations, it still remains a powerful film.

Other notable cinematic appearances have included *Command Decision, The War Lover, Tora! Tora! Tora!* (in which five of Aircraft Specialities' tankers appeared), *Memphis Belle* (the 1990 remake), one even made a brief appearance in the James Bond film *Thunderball*, and, without doubt, the best Fortress film of them all, Darryl F Zanuck's 1949 production of *Twelve O'Clock High*, which starred Gregory Peck and Dean Jagger. The latter featured a dozen B-17s – the last time this number of Fortresses would fly together.

Today, the charismatic B-17 still graces the sky in Europe and America, with some 14 airworthy examples flying on a regular basis. Others are due to join the ranks of 'flyers' as owners and operators lavish much tender loving care, not to mention large amounts of money, to keep these famous aerial icons of a bygone era operational for all to see.

Top right: A distinctive paint scheme to say the least! This, the 5,000th B-17 produced at Seattle following the Japanese attack at Pearl Harbor, was given the logo *5 Grand* and was signed by a huge number of Boeing employees. Strangely enough, it was allowed to keep these unusual markings and went on to take part in over 70 operational missions. (Boeing)

Left: B-17 crews of the 381st Bomb Group attend their briefing in readiness for *D-Day*. It was truly a maximum effort for all the Allied air forces on June 6, 1944. (US National Archives)

Below: Returning from a raid on the German ball-bearing factory at Steyr, Austria, on April 2, 1944, B-17G 42-38066 *Marishka* of the 97th Bomb Group is met by the station 'blood wagon' (ambulance) at Amendola Field, Italy. (Robert F Dorr)

Right: B-17E 41-9112 was equipped, for experimental purposes, with the nose and tail gun turrets from a Consolidated B-24 Liberator. There were also alterations made to the radio operator's roof hatch – note the open gun position and the cut-out portion at the base of the aircraft's rudder. Captured by the camera at Gander Airport, Newfoundland, in October 1943, the bomber had night-stopped to wait for the en-route weather to clear before flying on to Prestwick, UK. (Robert F Dorr)

Right: A formation of eight Flying Fortresses rumble over this B-17G, as its crew prepare to embark on another mission. Note the cover over the secret Norden bombsight in the nose. If cameras were present near the aircraft this vital piece of equipment was usually kept hidden from view. (US National Archives)

Left: Nose art adorned many B-17s, which saw operational service. *The Biggest Bird*, 43-38306, a B-17G of the 91st Bomb Group, US 8th Air Force, was decorated with a bomb-carrying Ostrich. (Robert F Dorr)

Opposite page, bottom left: The crew of B-17G *Button Nose* goes over the flight plan before boarding the bomber for another sortie over occupied territory. (US National Archives)

Opposite page, bottom right: The concentration of defensive fire from the close formations of Fortresses was originally thought to facilitate the bombers flying to and from their targets with fighter escort. Experience proved this was not to be the case and the 'little friends' were a much needed asset while over enemy occupied territory. Nevertheless instruction on how to fly a close formation was very much part of the USAAF's wartime training syllabus. Here Captain Jack Westward, a USAAF instructor, points out to a future B-17 crew the reasons for the staggered box formations flown by the 8th Air Force in Europe. (US National Archives)

Top right: The status board of the 401st Bomb Group, which was based at Deenethorpe, UK, between November 1943 to May 1945, is updated with the latest information in readiness for the next operation. (US National Archives)

Centre right: With a 'Bugs Bunny'-style rabbit adorning the nose, B-17F 'S for Sugar' of the 303rd Bomb Group is attended to by its ground crew. A multitude of tasks had to be carried out before a Fortress was ready to fly and fight and the groundcrews really were the unsung heroes of World War Two. (US National Archives)

Right: Dingy drill was sometimes looked on by aircrews as a boring exercise. However, if a bomber had to ditch in the water the skills gained during the interminable drills really proved their worth! (US National Archives)

Left: The US Coast Guard operated some 18 Flying Fortresses from the mid 1940s onwards. Fitted with an H2X radar radome in place of the chin turret, many of the Coast Guard aircraft also carried an airborne lifeboat for dropping to downed airmen. (Robert F Dorr)

Below: The Boeing XB-38 was an in-line-engined version of the B-17. Originally B-17E 41-2401, it was allocated, at the US Army Air Force's request, to the Lockheed-Vega factory for study into the possibility of fitting different engines to the airframe. Its four Wright R-1820-97 radials of 1,000hp (746kW) apiece were removed and replaced by a quartet of Allison V-1710-89 V-12 engines, each producing 1,425hp (1,063kW). Flying for the first time in its new configuration on May 19, 1943, its full potential could not be ascertained as the aircraft crashed on June 16 as the result of an engine fire, which could not be extinguished. Conversion work on two more XB-38s was subsequently cancelled. (Key Collection)

Left: Being a multi-engined aircraft, the B-17 proved to be a useful tool in post-war engine tests. Converted by Boeing – Wichita to carry a Wright R-3350 radial engine, B-17G 44-85813 (N6694C) had its cockpit moved 47in (0.12m) to the rear in order to maintain the aircraft's centre of gravity. (Robert F Dorr)

Bottom Some surplus B-17s found post-war use as ad-hoc cargo and fire bombing aircraft. B-17E 41-9210 had all of its military equipment removed, the gun turrets were faired over and it was pressed into service hauling freight in Bolivia. During the late 1980s and early 1990s it was dormant in Florida, USA, with the civil registration N8WJ. Since purchased by the recently-formed Washington DC-based Flying Heritage Collection, which intends to fly the bomber again, it has been re-registered as N12355 and is being put back into stock military condition. (Key - David Stephens Collection)

Above: A Flying Fortress bombardier checks his instrumentation before take off. Perched in the extreme nose position, this was a vulnerable spot to be in until the advent of the chin-located gun turret, which was fitted to the B-17G model. (US National Archives)

Top right: As with most bombers during World War Two, most of the work carried out on the aircraft took place in the open air. Only for major servicing did the four-engined 'heavies' see the interior of a hangar. Here, two members of a 92nd Bomb Group maintenance crew apply unit markings to the tail of a Flying Fortress. (US National Archives)

Right: *Flak* was an ever-present problem for the Allied bomber crews. Three members of B-17G *Peacemaker* inspect damage to the port wing. (US National Archives)

Below: B-17G *Pink Lady*, resplendent in 351st Bomb Group markings, is currently one of only two airworthy Fortresses in Europe. Formerly operated by the Institut Geographique National on worldwide survey flights it is now flown as a preserved airframe by the Fortresse Toujours Volante organisation of Paris, France. (Key – Duncan Cubitt)

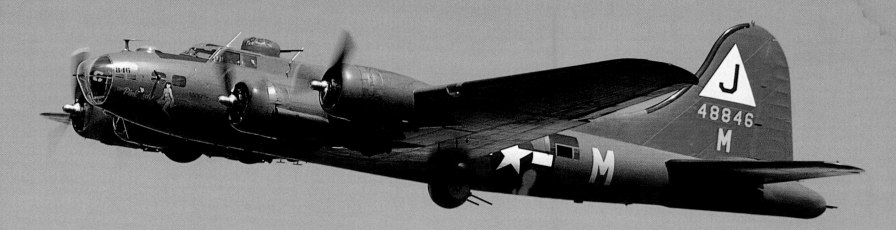

② FLYING FORTRESS IN DETAIL

Boeing's B-17 was, for its day, a complex aircraft. From its inception some of the higher echelons in the military voiced concerns over pilot capabilities to fly this large aircraft with its multifarious systems. Many were in favour of procuring larger numbers of less complicated designs, but in the end, the Flying Fortress reigned supreme, as it still does in the eyes of many.

On board the bomber was a host of separate crew stations and, on the whole, the interior was relatively roomy. Compared to cramped British bombers, such as the Avro Lancaster and Handley Page Halifax, the B-17 excelled in the amount of space available for crew members to carry out their jobs in reasonable conditions.

As with any fighting aircraft, improvements were made as the type entered and saw service with the military. It was found fairly early on in its career that the two waist gunners were restricted in their movement due to the windows being exactly opposite each other. This was remedied when the positions were staggered on later marks of the Fortress. This, and many other internal improvements made the B-17's interior a much more practical proposition for going to war.

Left: The heart of any aircraft is its cockpit. The 'office' of B-17G 44-83735 *Mary Alice* at the Imperial War Museum, Duxford, Cambs, UK, has been restored to its original configuration and does not feature any modern radios or navigational aids, which sometimes, by law, have to be fitted to the world's airworthy Fortresses. The two large control yokes, engine throttles, rudder pedals and multitude of wires, pipes and cabling are all evident in this illustration. *Mary Alice* – UK. (Key – Duncan Cubitt)

Lower left: The cockpit of Britain's airworthy B-17G, *Sally B*. Although *Mary Alice* and *Sally B* both came from the IGN in France, note the differences in cockpit layout. Propeller feathering switches are mounted on the top of the instrument panel coaming on *Sally B*, whereas on *Mary Alice* they are contained within the central instrument panel itself. *Sally B* is also fitted with a set of modern radio communications equipment, mounted to the left of the central panel. The blue rope around the control columns is not a standard fit, the bomber was undergoing its winter maintenance schedule when this photograph was taken and the rope was being used to restrain the aircraft's control surfaces! *Sally B* – UK. (Key – Steve Fletcher)

Above: Looking out either side of the cockpit the flightcrew are always aware of the four mighty Wright Cyclone R-1820 turbocharged radial engines, which collectively provide 4,800hp (3,580 kW). *Yankee Lady* – USA. (Key – Ken Delve)

Right: American designers tended to favour air-cooled radial engines for many aircraft types, which emanated from the USA during World War Two. While in-line, liquid-cooled engines had a more streamlined frontal area, they were more susceptible to overheating due to damage to the cooling system. Radials did not suffer the overheating problems, but they presented a 'blunt' frontal 'signature' which incurred more drag. *Yankee Lady* – USA. (Key – Duncan Cubitt)

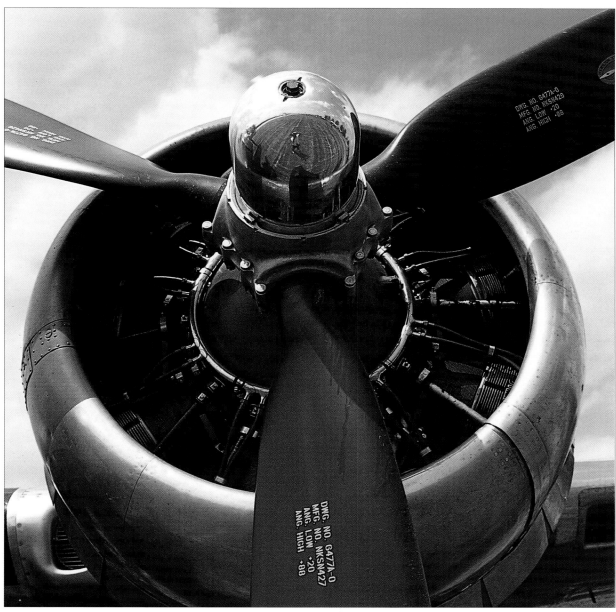

Left: Perched in the extreme nose behind this distinctive Perspex blister, was the bombardier. *Sally B* – UK. (Key – Steve Fletcher)

Right: Behind the bombardier sat the navigator, with his attendant maps, charts and direction-finding instruments. *Yankee Lady* – USA. (Key – Duncan Cubitt)

Above: Pictured in full operational garb, this B-17 navigator is seen plotting the route to the target. (US National Archives)

Below: With the bomb release gear mounted on the left wall, the bombardier's seat is perched directly atop the chin turret in this B-17G. In front of him is the famed Norden bombsight. The control column-style arrangement stowed on the right is the mechanism for controlling and firing the turret under the nose. *Yankee Lady* – USA. (Key – Duncan Cubitt)

Bottom right: Wartime photograph showing the inner workings of a B-17F's nose compartment. The entry and exit door to the rear of the compartment is accessible by means of a trapdoor just aft of the central instrument console in the cockpit. (Robert F Dorr)

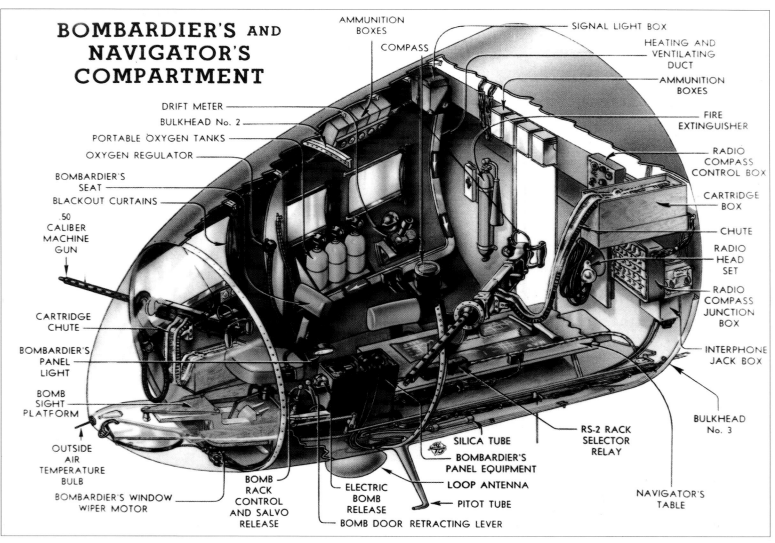

BOMBARDIER'S AND NAVIGATOR'S COMPARTMENT

AMMUNITION BOXES

COMPASS

SIGNAL LIGHT BOX

HEATING AND VENTILATING DUCT

AMMUNITION BOXES

DRIFT METER

BULKHEAD No. 2

PORTABLE OXYGEN TANKS

OXYGEN REGULATOR

FIRE EXTINGUISHER

RADIO COMPASS CONTROL BOX

BOMBARDIER'S SEAT

BLACKOUT CURTAINS

CARTRIDGE BOX

.50 CALIBER MACHINE GUN

CHUTE

RADIO HEAD SET

CARTRIDGE CHUTE

RADIO COMPASS JUNCTION BOX

BOMBARDIER'S PANEL LIGHT

INTERPHONE JACK BOX

BOMB SIGHT PLATFORM

BULKHEAD No. 3

OUTSIDE AIR TEMPERATURE BULB

SILICA TUBE

BOMBARDIER'S PANEL EQUIPMENT

RS-2 RACK SELECTOR RELAY

BOMBARDIER'S WINDOW WIPER MOTOR

BOMB RACK CONTROL AND SALVO RELEASE

ELECTRIC BOMB RELEASE

LOOP ANTENNA

PITOT TUBE

NAVIGATOR'S TABLE

BOMB DOOR RETRACTING LEVER

Left: Immediately behind the pilot and co-pilot was the upper gun turret. With no seat available to sit on, the gunner stood on the protruding steps on the left and right in order to elevate himself into the turret cupola. The six grey boxes on either side of the turret mechanism were used to house the belts of ammunition to feed the guns. *Yankee Lady* – USA. (Key – Duncan Cubitt)

Top right: Aft of the upper gun turret was the B-17's relatively small bomb-bay. With only a narrow walkway and two guide ropes to hold on to, this was not an area to be in when the bomb doors were open! *Mary Alice* – UK. (Key – Duncan Cubitt)

Bottom right: The B-17's radio operator was positioned aft and to the right of the bomb-bay, with only a thin wooden door separating him from several thousand pounds of high explosive! *Yankee Lady* – USA. (Key – Duncan Cubitt)

Below: The bombardier and navigator also doubled up as front gunners when required, using the two forward fuselage-mounted .50 calibre machine guns. *Yankee Lady* – USA. (Key – Duncan Cubitt)

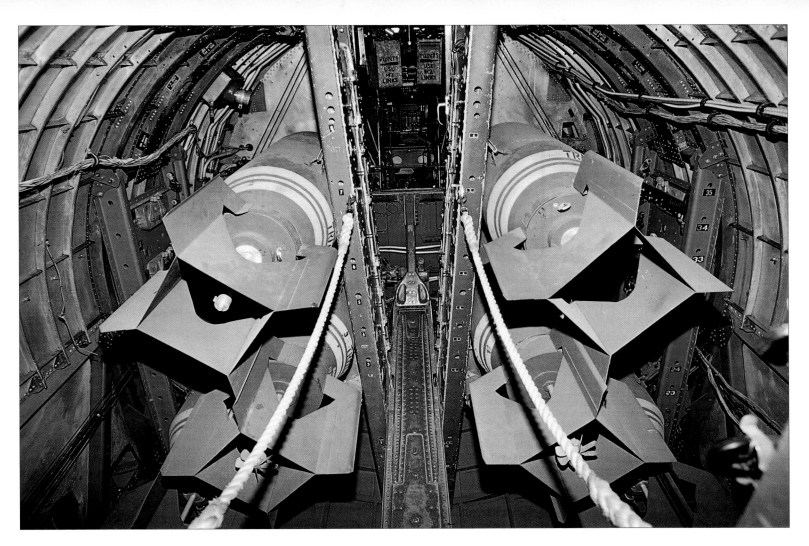

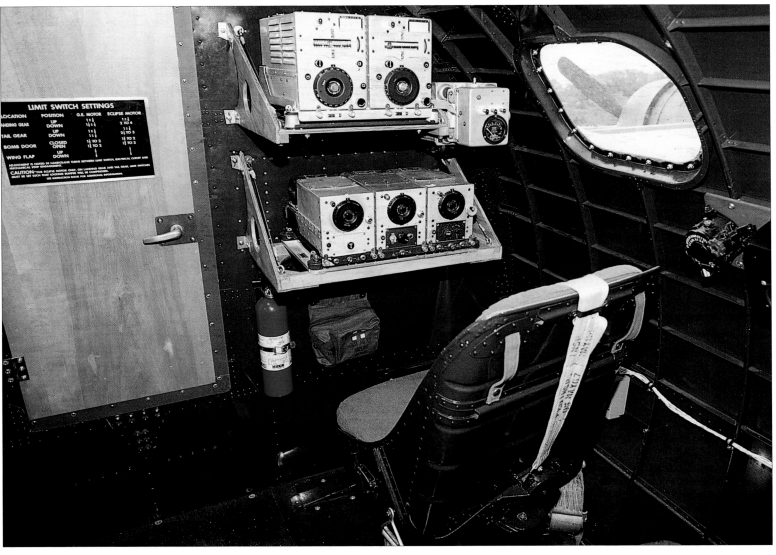

Top left: Looking forward from the crew entry door, the proximity of the waist guns to the ball turret can clearly be seen. The wooden boxes seen attached to the fuselage walls carry the ammunition for the two machine-guns. *Mary Alice* – UK. (Key – Steve Fletcher)

Above: The notorious ball turret. Even though this was a small affair, it, and its workings, took up a fair amount of space in the B-17's rear fuselage. The raised walkway can be seen to the left of the fuselage and was the sole means of getting past the turret to access the forward sections of the bomber. *Sally B* – UK. (Key – Steve Fletcher)

Left: After a period of retaliation against enemy fighters the inside of the B-17s rear fuselage could swiftly become awash with the spent cartridge cases from the two waist machine guns. (US National Archives)

Opposite page top: Gunners occupying the ball turret were usually of small stature, as the space inside the .50 calibre-equipped sphere was severely limited. Note the oblong slots in the casing just below the gun barrels, used for dumping the spent cartridges. *Yankee Lady* – USA. (Key – Duncan Cubitt)

Opposite page bottom: Upon entering the B-17 from the rear door, and looking left, the tailwheel strut can be seen aft of the fuselage walkway. The bomber's tail turret was accessed by way of a small door, to the rear of the tail assembly. *Yankee Lady* – USA. (Key – Duncan Cubitt)

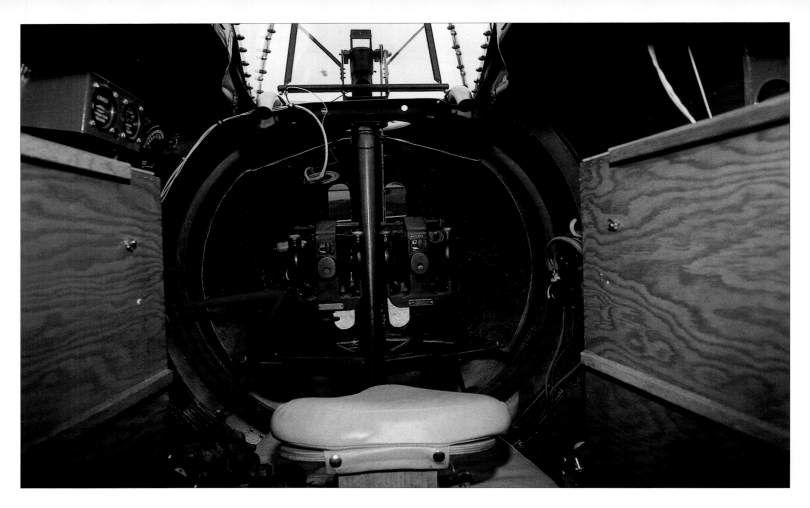

Above: Like the ball turret, the rear gun position was not one to be in if you had a phobia for enclosed spaces. With only a small seat to sit on and little access to the rest of the aircraft, the rear gunner was literally out on a limb from the rest of the crew and could only communicate via the intercom. *Yankee Lady* – USA. (Key – Duncan Cubitt)

Below: Charged with protecting the rear of the B-17, the tail gunner had very little protection and had to peer out of this small area of Perspex. Perched at the extreme rear of the Fortress, it was indeed a daunting task. *Mary Alice* – UK. (Key – Duncan Cubitt)

Above: Illustrating the World War Two period combat clothing, several living history groups throughout Europe and the USA give a feel of what adorned wartime bomber crews. This 'crew' positioned itself alongside the Confederate Air Force's B-17G *Texas Raiders* at Minneapolis in 1995. (Key – Duncan Cubitt)

Below: The starboard waist gun position on the Imperial War Museum's static B-17G. Often to get a better field of fire the gunners would remove the Perspex, thereby totally exposing themselves to the elements. *Mary Alice* – UK. (Key – Steve Fletcher)

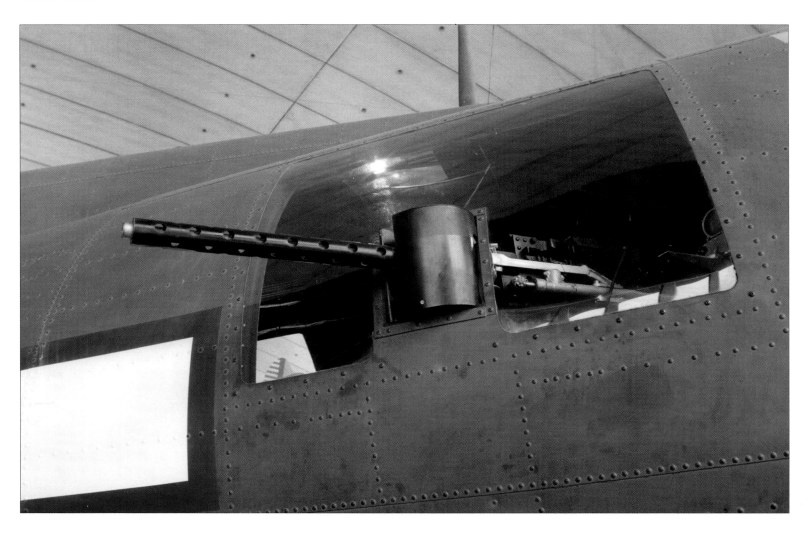

Left: The B-17's undercarriage assembly comprised one major strut, which took the weight of the aircraft, with retraction being made possible by electric motors that activated screw jacks to bring the wheel up into the undercarriage bay. When fully retracted the lower half of the wheel hung down in the slipstream, thereby (in theory) affording some protection to the rest of the airframe if a wheels-up landing had to be undertaken. *Mary Alice* – UK. (Key – Steve Fletcher)

Below: Taking a look at a B-17 which is undergoing winter maintenance or restoration to flying condition affords many viewpoints which serve to illustrate just how complex this aircraft was for its day. Even in this new millennium it remains an enormous undertaking to keep one of these 'heavies' in the air. *Sally B* – UK. (Key – Steve Fletcher)

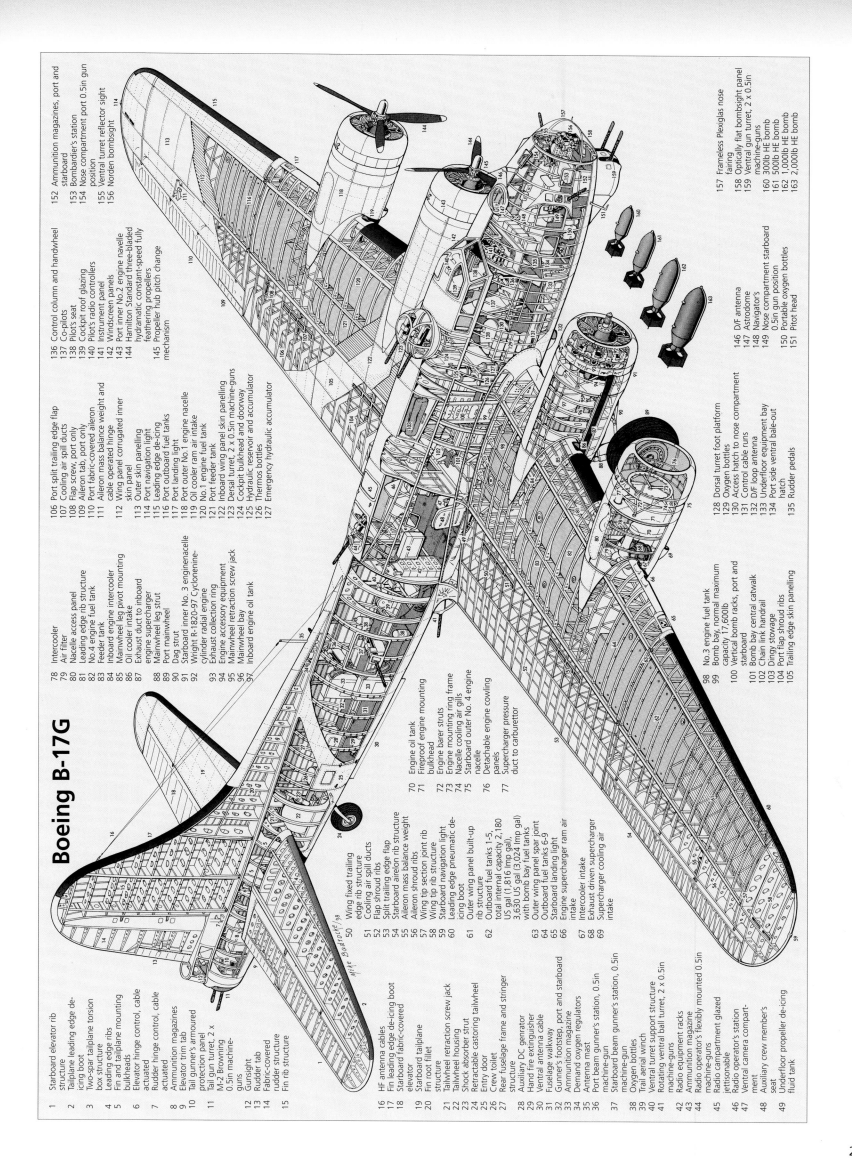

Boeing B-17G

1 Starboard elevator rib structure
2 Tailplane leading edge de-icing boot
3 Two-spar tailplane torsion box structure
4 Leading edge ribs
5 Fin and tailplane mounting bulkheads
6 Elevator hinge control, cable actuated
7 Rudder hinge control, cable actuated
8 Ammunition magazines
9 Tail gunner's armoured protection panel
10 Tail gun turret, 2 x M-2 Browning 0.5in machine-guns
11 Gunsight
12 Rudder tab
13 Elevator trim tab
14 Fabric-covered rudder structure
15 Fin rib structure
16 HF antenna cables
17 Fin leading edge de-icing boot
18 Starboard fabric-covered elevator
19 Starboard tailplane
20 Fin root fillet structure
21 Tailwheel retraction screw jack
22 Tailwheel housing
23 Shock absorber strut
24 Retractable castoring tailwheel
25 Entry door
26 Crew toilet
27 Rear fuselage frame and stringer structure
28 Auxiliary DC genrator
29 Hand fire extinguisher
30 Ventral antenna cable
31 Fuselage walkway
32 Gunner's footstep, port and starboard
33 Demand oxygen regulators
34 Ammunition magazine
35 Antenna mast
36 Radio operator's flexibly mounted 0.5in machine-gun
37 Starboard beam gunner's station, 0.5in machine-gun
38 Oxygen bottles
39 Trail aerial winch
40 Ventral turret support structure
41 Rotating ventral ball turret, 2 x 0.5in machine-guns
42 Radio equipment racks
43 Ammunition magazine
44 Radio operator's seat
45 Radio compartment glazed jettisonable
46 Radio operator's station
47 Ventral camera compart-ment
48 Auxiliary crew member's seat
49 Underfloor propeller de-icing fluid tank

50 Wing fixed trailing edge rib structure
51 Cooling air spill ducts
52 Split trailing edge flap
53 Flap shroud structure
54 Starboard airelon rib structure
55 Aileron shroud ribs
56 Aileron mass balance weight
57 Wing tip section ribs
58 Wing tip rib structure
59 Starboard navigation light
60 Leading edge pneumatic de-icing boot
61 Outer wing panel built-up rib structure
62 Outboard fuel tanks 1-5, total internal capacity 2,180 US gal (1,816 Imp gal), 3,630 US gal (3,024 Imp gal) with bomb bay fuel tanks
63 Outer wing panel spar joint
64 Outboard fuel tanks 6-9
65 Starboard landing light
66 Engine supercharger ram air intake
67 Intercooler intake
68 Exhaust driven supercharger
69 Supercharger cooling air intake
70 Engine oil tank
71 Fireproof engine mounting bulkhead
72 Engine barer struts
73 Engine mounting ring frame
74 Nacelle cooling air gills
75 Starboard outer No. 4 engine nacelle
76 Detachable engine cowling panels
77 Supercharger pressure duct to carburettor
78 Intercooler
79 Air filter
80 Nacelle access panel
81 Leading edge rib structure
82 No.4 engine fuel tank
83 Feeder tank
84 Inboard engine intercooler
85 Mainwheel leg pivot mounting
86 Oil cooler intake
87 Exhaust duct to inboard engine supercharger
88 Mainwheel leg strut
89 Port mainwheel
90 Dag strut
91 Starboard inner No. 3 enginenacelle
92 Wright R-1820-97 Cyclonenine-cylinder radial engine
93 Exhaust collection ring
94 Engine accessory equipment
95 Mainwheel retraction screw jack
96 Mainwheel bay
97 Inboard engine oil tank

98 No.3 engine fuel tank
99 Bomb bay, normal maximum capacity 17,600lb
100 Vertical bomb racks, port and starboard
101 Bomb bay central catwalk
102 Chain link handrail
103 Dingy stowage
104 Port flap shroud ribs
105 Trailing edge skin panelling
106 Port split trailing edge flap
107 Cooling air spill ducts
108 Flap screw, port only
109 Aileron tab, port only
110 Port fabric-covered aileron
111 Aileron mass balance weight and cable operated hinge
112 Wing panel corrugated inner skin panel
113 Outer skin panelling
114 Port navigation light
115 Leading edge de-icing
116 Port outboard fuel tanks
117 Port landing light
118 Port outer No.1 engine nacelle
119 Oil cooler ram air intake
120 No.1 engine fuel tank
121 Port feeder tank
122 Inboard wing panel skin panelling
123 Dersal turret, 2 x 0.5in machine-guns
124 Cockpit bulkhead and doorway
125 Hydraulic reservoir and accumulator
126 Thermos bottles
127 Emergency hydraulic accumulator

128 Dorsal turret foot platform
129 Oxygen bottles
130 Access hatch to nose compartment
131 Control cable runs
132 D/F loop antenna
133 Underfloor equipment bay
134 Port side ventral bale-out hatch
135 Rudder pedals
136 Control column and handwheel
137 Co-pilots
138 Pilot's seat
139 Cockpit roof glazing
140 Pilot's radio controllers
141 Instrument panel
142 Windscreen panels
143 Port inner No.2 engine navelle
144 Hamilton Standard three-bladed hydramatic constant-speed fully feathering propellers
145 Propeller hub pitch change mechanism
146 D/F antenna
147 Astrodome
148 Navigator's
149 Nose compartment starboard 0.5in gun position
150 Portable oxygen bottles
151 Pitot head
152 Ammunition magazines, port and starboard
153 Bombardier's station
154 Nose compartment port 0.5in gun position
155 Ventral turret reflector sight
156 Norden bombsight
157 Frameless Plexiglas nose fairing
158 Optically flat bombsight panel
159 Ventral gun turret, 2 x 0.5in machine-guns
160 300lb HE bomb
161 500lb HE bomb
162 1,000lb HE bomb
163 2,000lb HE bomb

THE FORTRESS COULD TAKE IT

Boeing's B-17 was a resilient aircraft. It had to be to cope with the rigours of aerial combat, which would be inflicted upon it during its service career. It was not uncommon for a Fortress to lose major portions of the airframe due to flak damage or enemy aircraft action, and still be able to return to base, albeit sometimes with difficulty. Engines not functioning, undercarriages which would not lower, ailerons, rudder and elevators missing, all of these scenarios afflicted Flying Fortresses, almost on a daily basis during World War Two.

Left: B-17G 42-37721 *Sugar* of the 534th Bomb Squadron, 381st Bomb Group, was based at Ridgewell from October 1943, but was damaged due to a wheels-up landing when it returned to base on December 22, no doubt as a result of enemy action. Jacked up and positioned on this temporary platform, the bomber was then moved to the airfield's maintenance area for repairs. (US National Archives)

Right: Not all damage was caused by the enemy. This B-17F was destroyed when its load of 500lb (226kg) bombs exploded, on May 28, 1943. (US National Archives)

Left: Fortress 'LL-Y' *Old Ironsides* of the Bassingbourn-based 91st Bomb Group returned home minus its entire starboard tailplane and elevator. The offending items were knocked off by a falling bomb from another B-17 of the 91st during a raid on Bremen. Needless to say that it took all of the pilot's skill to effect a safe return home! (US National Archives)

Right: After suffering a wheels-up landing, this B-17G has been temporarily parked on the edge of the airfield while its fate is decided. (Key collection)

Left: USAAF and Royal Air Force personnel inspect the damage to the nose of this B-17G of the 379th Bomb Group after a mission on June 28, 1944. The mechanism for operating the chin turret can still be seen in situ. (US National Archives)

Left: After being hit by a falling bomb, this B-17G had to undergo major repairs at its Ridgewell base. (US National Archives)

Right: *General Ike*, a B-17G of the 91st Bomb Group, lost its starboard inner propeller due to flak on its 65th mission. Unfortunately the wartime censor has all but obliterated the nose-art likeness of General Dwight D Eisenhower and the large gash in the aircraft's skin adjacent to the engine nacelle. (US National Archives)

Middle right: This 401st Bomb Group B-17G, 43-38125, looks somewhat worse for wear after its crash landing at Deenethorpe. The aircraft subsequently caught fire and was destroyed. (Key collection)

Bottom right: A truly amazing sight! This B-17 41-24406 *All American* is testament to the inherent strength of the Fortresses design. Struck by a Messerschmitt Bf 109 during an attack on Tunis in February 1941, the bomber's tail section was almost severed by the impact, which also knocked off the port tailplane, during the collision with the fighter. After the tail gunner had carefully crawled forward past the gash in the fuselage, the B-17 flew on to Biskra, where it landed safely. It is reported that shortly after landing the tail section of the aircraft fell off! However, that is not the end of the story, as the Fortress was given a replacement tail section and was subsequently used as a squadron 'hack' aircraft. (Boeing)

Left: One member of the groundcrew stands in the hole where the ball turret used to be, while two of the aircraft's aircrew survey the flak damage to this B-17 of the 351st Bomb Group. (US National Archives)

B-17 OPERATIONAL BOMBARDMENT GROUPS

A Bombardment Group normally had four permanently-assigned squadrons and operations were conducted on a Group basis. Aircraft complement of a Bombardment Squadron was eight in 1942, then raised to nine and to 14 late the following year. With reserves, 16 to 18 aircraft was the usual strength by the end of hostilities. This directory covers only Bombardment Groups involved in bombing operations. B-17s were employed by a number of other groups and independent squadrons in special operational activities. Compiled with the best information available, every effort has been made to illustrate a representative selection of aircraft from as many of the Bomb Groups as possible.

2nd Bombardment Group

Squadrons	20th, 49th, 96th and 429th BS
Assignment	12th AF and 15th AF
Models	B-17F and G
Op Period	April 1943 to May 1945
Bases	Navarin, Chateaudun-du-Rhumel and Ain M'lila, Algeria; Massicault and Bizerte, Tunisia; Amendola and Foggia, Italy
Losses	176 MIA

5th Bombardment Group

Squadrons	23rd, 31st, 72nd and 394th BS
Assignment	7th AF, 13th AF
Models	B-17D, E and F (Converted to B-24)
Op Period	December 1941 to September 1943
Bases	Hickam, Hawaii; Espiritu Santo, New Hebrides; Guadalcanal, Solomon Islands
Losses	15 MIA

Located in the Hawaiian Islands the 5th operated B-17Ds and Douglas B-18 Bolos in the early part of World War Two. During the Japanese attack on Pearl Harbor the unit lost many of its aircraft, while based at Hickam Field. Following America's entry into the war, the 5th mounted patrol missions around the Hawaiian Islands, until 1942, when it relocated to Espiritu Santo in the Soloman Islands. While based there it flew a mixture of B-17s and B-14s, participating, as part of the 13th AF, in the Soloman and Philippine campaigns. At the end of the war it remained based in the area, but by 1947 had been deactivated.

7th Bombardment Group

Squadrons	9th, 11th, 22nd and 436th BS
Assignment	10th AF
Models	B-17E
Op Period	December 1941 to November 1942 (Converted to B-24)
Bases	Brisbane, Australia; Karachi and Dum-Dum, India
Losses	8 MIA

It was six of this group's B-17Es which arrived at Pearl Harbor during the Japanese attack. Taking evasive action and landing at other airfields, they somehow managed to survive the devastation being wrought on the American installations. Subsequently operating from Java the group carried out attacks on Japanese airfields, shipping and facilities in the Philippines and the Netherlands East Indies. After the American surrender in March 1942 the 7th BG was transferred to India where it was attached to the 10th Air Force. Continuing to operate against the Japanese, by the end of the war conversion to the B-24 Liberator was imminent.

11th Bombardment Group

Squadrons	26th, 42nd, 98th and 431st BS
Assignment	7th AF, 13th AF
Models	B-17D, E and F
Op Period	December 1941 to March 1943. (Converted to B-24)
Bases	Wheeler, Hawaii; Efate and Espiritu Santo, New Hebrides
Losses	24 MIA

Following patrol missions around the Hawaiian area as a result of the Japanese attack on Pearl Harbor, the 11th moved on to Midway Island as a result of intelligence reports which predicted an attack by the Japanese. Used to fly missions against enemy shipping during the Battle of Midway, the group subsequently moved to the New Hebrides in July 1942. Operating against enemy airfields in the Soloman Islands until 1942, the unit then returned to the USA for conversion to Liberators.

Below: A staged propaganda photograph in the early part of the B-17's military career shows a pair of B-17Es, both of which were scheduled to fly out to the Philippines to supplement the embattled 19th Bomb Group. However, they were instead diverted to Java and served with the 7th Bomb Group in the courageous, but hopeless holding action. Both aircraft are fitted with the short-lived, remotely-operated ventral gun position. (Robert F Dorr)

Below: This B-17D, 40-3097, *The Swoose*, part of the 14th Bomb Squadron, 19th Bomb Group, was the last survivor of the Japanese attack on Clark Field, Manila, which took place on December 8, 1941, the day after the attack on Pearl Harbor. After taking part in many operational sorties it returned to the USA in 1942 and is now undergoing preservation at the National Air & Space Museum's facility at Suitland, USA. (Pete West)

Below: B-17E *Tojo's Jinx* was one of the Flying Fortresses flown to Australia in 1942 to aid the units which at that time were withdrawing from the Philippines and Java. Note the toned down red portion of the national insignia on the aircraft's fuselage, compared to *The Swoose*. This was carried out to prevent any confusion with the Japanese national insignia. (Pete West)

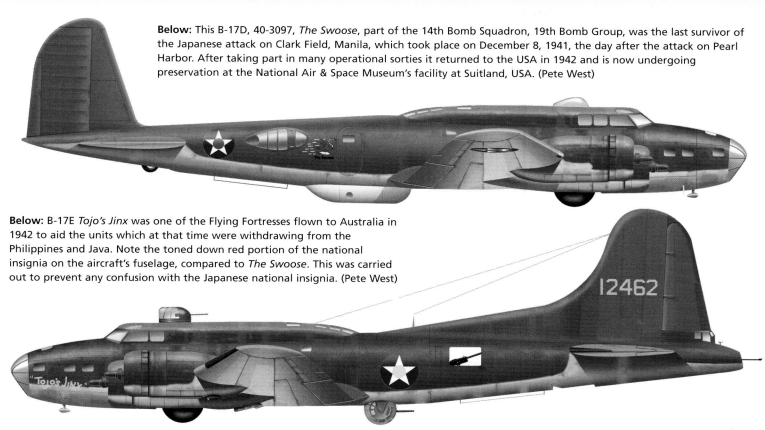

91st BG

Bottom left: The 9th Bomb Squadron, 7th Bomb Group flew B-17Es from Singosari Airfield, near Malang, Java, during the ill-fated struggle to retain the area. Operating in rough conditions, the Fortresses used British-made 749lb (340kg) bombs to prosecute their war. On January 20, 1942, Japanese fighters strafed Singosari and destroyed five B-17s, although 41-2499, illustrated here, managed to escape the ravages of the attack. Note the pre-war US national insignia on the fuselage, which was used throughout the Java campaign. (Robert F Dorr)

19th Bombardment Group	
Squadrons	14th, 28th, 30th, 93rd and 435th BS
Models	B-17C, D and E
Assignment	5th AF
Op Period	December 1941 to December 1942. (Returned to USA)
Bases	Clark, Luzon; Batchelor, Australia; Singosari, Java; Melbourne, Garbutt, Longreach and Mareeba, Australia
Losses	18 MIA

Another unit which was based in the Philippines at the outbreak of World War Two, the 19th lost a large number of aircraft while trying to repel the advancing Japanese forces. Remnants of the group then flew to Australia, but by the end of 1941 relocated to Java, where attacks were mounted against the Japanese, as well as rescuing General MacArthur and his staff as the Philippines capitulated. Taking part in the Battle of the Coral Sea, the 19th also saw action in New Guinea. By 1942 it was reassigned to the USA as a training unit before converting on tothe B-29 Superfortress in April 1944.

34th Bombardment Group	
Squadrons	4th, 7th, 18th and 391st BS
Assignment	8th AF
Models	B-17G
Op Period	October 1944 to May 1945 (Converted from B-24)
Bases	Mendlesham, UK
Losses	15 MIA

The oldest USAAF Bomb Group to serve with the 8th Air Force, the 34th BG was activated at Langley Field, Virginia, on January 15, 1941. Initially flying B-24 Liberators on anti-submarine patrols and training exercises, the air echelon of the 34th took the southern ferry route to the UK, starting from Florida on March 31, 1944. Its first operational

mission in the European Theatre of Operations (ETO) took place on May 23, 1944, when the unit was still equipped with Liberators. B-17Gs took over from September 17, 1944, serving operationally until the 34th returned to the USA in June/July 1945. Flying a total of 170 missions, 62 of which were with the B-24, the 34th never lost an aircraft to fighter action over enemy territory. The only losses to enemy aircraft were over its own base in the UK!

43rd Bombardment Group	
Squadrons	63rd, 64th, 65th and 403rd BS
Assignment	5th AF
Models	B-17E and F
Op Period	August 1942 to September 1943 (Converted to B-24)
Bases	Sydney and Torrens Creek, Australia; Port Morseby, New Guinea
Losses	10 MIA

The 43rd BG joined the 5th AF in March 1942, operating in the Pacific region. Flying anti-shipping patrols the group was responsible for the destruction of a Japanese shipping convoy in the Bismarck Sea during March 1943. During May to September 1943 conversion to the B-24 took place.

91st Bombardment Group	
Squadrons	32nd, 323rd, 324th and 401st BS
Assignment	8th AF
Models	B-17F and G
Op Period	November 1942 to May 1945
Bases	Kimbolton September 12 to October 13, 1942
	Bassingbourn October 14, 1942 to June 23, 1945
Losses	197 MIA

Known as the 'Ragged Irregulars' the 91st BG underwent training in the US from April 1942 until its departure for

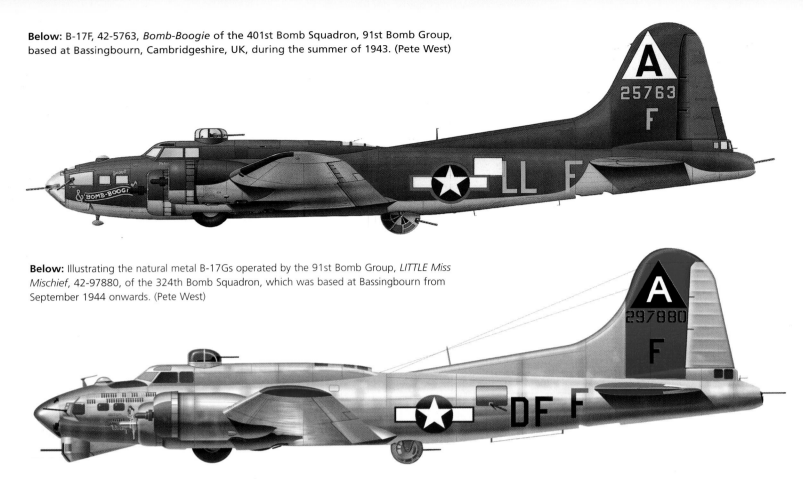

Below: B-17F, 42-5763, *Bomb-Boogie* of the 401st Bomb Squadron, 91st Bomb Group, based at Bassingbourn, Cambridgeshire, UK, during the summer of 1943. (Pete West)

Below: Illustrating the natural metal B-17Gs operated by the 91st Bomb Group, *LITTLE Miss Mischief*, 42-97880, of the 324th Bomb Squadron, which was based at Bassingbourn from September 1944 onwards. (Pete West)

the UK in September, the ground echelon boarding the *Queen Mary* while the air echelon waited at Gowen Field, Idaho for enough new B-17Fs to be assigned. The first squadron deployed across the Atlantic in·late September and by mid October most were in place. The unit established itself at Bassingbourn where it remained throughout the war. The first operational mission was flown on November 7, 1942 with 14 aircraft joining a small force of B-17s and B-24s attacking U-boat pens at Brest in France. Five of the unit's aircraft were damaged and five crewmen wounded. Between then and the Group's last mission on April 25, 1945 it flew 9,591 sorties for the loss of 197 aircraft (the highest loss rate of any of the 8th Air Force bomber Groups). The unit's most famous aircraft was *Nine-O-Nine*, which completed 140 missions without a turn back. An 8th AF record!

92nd Bombardment Group

Squadrons	325th, 326th, 327th and 407th BS
Assignment	8th AF
Models	B-17E, F, G and YB-40
Op Period	September 1942 to May 1945
Bases	Bovingdon, Alconbury and Podington, UK
Losses	154 MIA

This was the first Bomb Group to make a non-stop Atlantic flight from the USA to the UK and the Group which led the last 8th AF mission of World War Two. The 92nd BG, 'Fame's Favoured Few', flew a total of 8,633 sorties in 308 missions, dropping an impressive 20,829 tons of bombs during the course of its deployment to the UK. The 326th BS was the only unit to be equipped with the YB-40 (a conversion of the B-17F to test the heavily

armed bomber escort concept) for combat. Between August 1942 and May 1943 the 92nd BG acted as the 8th AF's Combat Crew Replacement Centre.

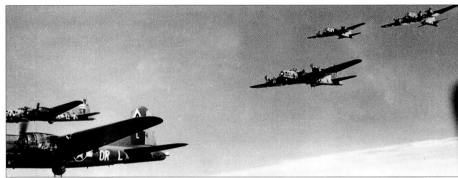

94th Bombardment Group

Squadrons	331st, 332nd, 333rd and 410th BS
Assignment	8th AF
Models	B-17F and G
Op Period	May 1943 to May 1945
Bases	Bassingbourn April to May 27, 1943
	Earls Colne May 12 to June 13, 1943
	Bury St Edmunds June 13, 1943 to December 12, 1945
Losses	153 MIA

92nd BG

94th BG

Above 42-30383, *Brennan's Circus*, an un-coded B-17F of the 94th Bomb Group accompanies another Fortress from the same Group. (US National Archives)

Top right: One of the 96th Bomb Group's B-17Gs pictured near Budapest during the second Russian shuttle raid in September 1944. (Key Collection)

Left: A section of 323rd and 401st Bomb Squadron/91st BG B-17Fs coded 'OR' and 'LL' display the Group's letter A encased in a triangle, superimposed on an 80in (203cm) wide vertical red band on the fin. (US National Archives)

Left: A pair of 324th Bomb Squadron, 91st Bomb Group, 'DF'-coded B-17Fs head out towards enemy territory on yet another 8th Air Force raid. (US National Archives)

Formed at McDill in Florida in June 1942 the 94th BG completed its initial training at various air bases before moving to the UK in April 1943. The Group's first mission was flown on May 13, 1943 when, as part of the 4th Bombardment Wing, it sent 21 bombers to attack industrial targets at Antwerp, losing one aircraft. Having flown 8,884 sorties in 324 missions the Group remained in the UK until the end of 1945 before returning to the US to be disbanded.

95th Bombardment Group	
Squadrons	334th, 335th, 336th and 412th BS
Assignment	8th AF
Models	B-17F and G
Op Period	May 1943 to May 1945
Bases	Alconbury, Framlingham and Horham, UK
Losses	157 MIA

Taking the southern route from Florida, via Trinidad, Brazil and Dakar, aircraft of the 95th BG arrived in the UK in April 1943. It was the only 8th AF unit to be awarded three Distinguished Unit Citations, for attacks on Regensburg, Munster and Berlin. The 95th also held the highest total claims of enemy aircraft destroyed (425) of all bomb groups within the 8th AF and was the first USAAF group to bomb Berlin, a task it undertook on March 4, 1944.

96th Bombardment Group	
Squadrons	337th, 338th, 339th and 413th BS
Assignment	8th AF
Models	B-17F and G
Op Period	May 1943 to May 1945
Bases	Grafton Underwood, Great Saling and Snetterton Heath, UK
Losses	189 MIA

Suffering the second highest missing-in-action loss rate of any of the 8th AF's groups, the 96th arrived in the UK in mid-April, 1943, and went on to lead the first shuttle mission, Regensburg – Africa, on August 17, 1943. Carrying out some 8,924 sorties in 321 missions, the 96th dropped 19,277 tons of bombs before being redeployed to the USA in November 1945.

95th BG

96th BG

Below: With its 'Mickey' H2S radome shown in its fully extended position (these replaced the more usual ball turret), this 413rd Bomb Squadron, 96th Bomb Group, pathfinder aircraft wears the natural metal finish seen on the bulk of Flying Fortresses during the later stages of World War Two. (Pete West)

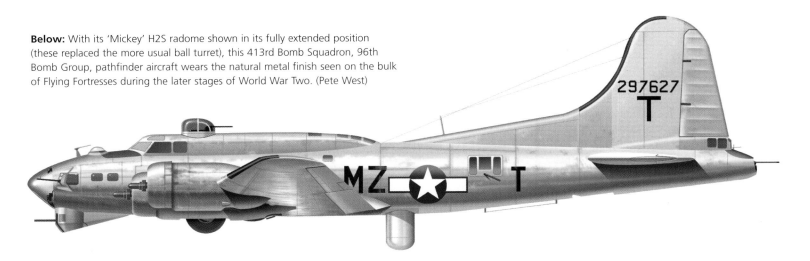

97th Bombardment Group	
Squadrons	340th, 341st, 342nd and 414th BS
Assignment	8th AF, 12th AF and 15th AF
Models	B-17E, F and G
Op Period	August 1942 to May 1945
Bases	Polebrook, Grafton Underwood, UK; Maison Blanche, Tafaraoui, Biskra and Chateaudun-du-Rhumel, Algeria; Pont-du-Fahs and Depienne, Tunisia; Cerignola and Amendola, Italy
Losses	124 MIA

Flying the 8th AF's first heavy bomber mission from the UK, on August 17, 1942, the 97th arrived in the ETO in July 1942. Its stay in England was relatively short. It was deployed to North Africa in November 1942 after only 14 missions, during which it dropped 395 tons of bombs. As part of the 15th AF it flew the first shuttle mission from Italy to Russia as well as attacking targets in southern Germany and the Balkans.

99th Bombardment Group	
Squadrons	346th, 347th, 348th and 416th BS
Assignment	12th AF and 15th AF
Models	B-17F and G
Op Period	March 1943 to May 1945
Bases	Navarin, Algeria; Oudna, Tunisia and Tortorella, Italy
Losses	98 MIA

Moving to North Africa from February 1942 and May 1943, after training in the USA, the 99th was used in the 'softening up' process prior to the Allied attacks on the Italian peninsula. Moving on to Italy, the unit was initially based at Tortorella Airfield, near Foggia, where it was used in attacks on strategic targets, which included the

Messerschmitt Bf 109 factory at Weiner Neustadt. The 99th was disbanded in Italy in November 1945.

100th Bombardment Group	
Squadrons	349th, 350th, 351st and 418th BS
Assignment	8th AF
Models	B-17F and G
Op Period	June 1943 to May 1945
Bases	Podington, June 2 to 8, 1943 Thorpe Abbotts, June 9, 1943 to December 1945
Losses	177 MIA

One of the best-known bomber groups, partly because of it name – the 'Bloody Hundredth' – this Group formed in Florida in June 1942 and arrived in the UK in May the following year. The first mission, June 25, 1943 was as part of a 78 B-17 formation attacking a convoy off Juist Island. Only two of the Group's 19 aircraft made an effective attack but three aircraft were lost. The 'Bloody Hundredth's' reputation for heavy losses thus started on day one. To the end of the war the unit lost 177 aircraft missing in action with a further 52 operational losses – this from 8,630 sorties.

301st Bombardment Group	
Squadrons	32nd, 352nd, 353rd and 419th BS
Assignment	8th AF, 12th AF and 15th AF
Models	B-17F and G
Op Period	September 1942 to May 1945
Bases	Chelveston, UK; Tafaraoui, Masion Blanche, Biskra, Ain M'lila, St Donat, Algeria; Oudna, Tunisia; Cerignola and Lucera, Italy
Losses	147 MIA

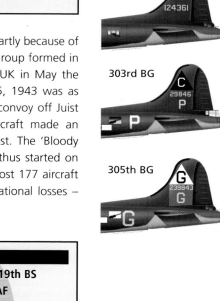

97th BG

100th BG

301st BG

303rd BG

305th BG

Left: After flak had damaged this 99th Bomb Group, 15th Air Force's B-17G's brakes and electrical system, the tail gunner made a novel use of his parachute to arrest the bomber's landing run. Note the deflated starboard undercarriage tyre. (US National Archives)

Left: A 351st Bomb Squadron, 100th Bomb Group, B-17G sits under a covering of snow at Thorpe Abbotts during the winter of 1944/45. Even during these harsh conditions, aircraft were maintained in the open, only seeing the inside of a hangar for major servicing or substantial repairs. (US National Archives)

Below: This Boeing-built B-17G of the 353rd Bomb Squadron, 301st Bomb Group wears 15th Air Force markings, which depict the period when the aircraft operated in Italy. (Pete West)

Below: 'Somewhere in England', as the propaganda captions used to say during World War Two. Sheltering among the trees at Molesworth is one of the 303rd Bomb Groups B-17Fs. (US National Archives)

Below right: A large crowd gathers to see the graffiti-ridden B-17F 41-24577 *Hells Angels* (the first B-17 to complete 25 missions in the ETO) of the 358th Bomb Squadron, 303rd Bomb Group, taxi out from Molesworth for another sortie against the enemy. (US National Archives)

This is another Group whose duty in the UK was short. It arrived in July, 1942, and stayed until November 1942, when it was sent to North Africa. During this time 104 sorties were mounted for the loss of just one aircraft. Transferred to the 12th AF, the 96th then operated in the Mediterranean theatre and later with the 15th AF in Italy.

303rd Bombardment Group	
Squadrons	358th, 359th, 360th and 427th BS
Assignment	8th AF
Models	B-17F and G
Op Period	November 1942 to May 1945
Bases	Molesworth, UK
Losses	165 MIA

This Group holds a number of impressive records – first 8th AF BG to complete 300 missions from the UK, first B-17 (*Hell's Angels*) to complete 25 missions in the ETO and first B-17 (*Knock Out Dropper*) in 8th AF to complete 50 and 75 missions. All of this was in addition to being the B-17 Group which flew more missions than any other. From November 17, 1942 through to April 25, 1945 the

303rd flew a staggering 10,721 sorties dropping 24,918 tons of bombs, plus 176 tons of leaflets. Subsequently used to transport troops from Europe to North Africa, the unit was moved to Casablanca at the end of May 1945, to join the North African Division, Air Transport Command, but was not required and as a result was inactivated in July 1945.

305th Bombardment Group	
Squadrons	364th, 365th, 366th and 422nd BS
Assignment	8th AF
Models	B-17F and G
Op Period	November 1942 to May 1945
Bases	Grafton Underwood and Chelveston, UK
Losses	154 MIA

Activated at Salt Lake City, Utah, USA, on March 1, 1942, and, under the initial leadership of Colonel Curtis LeMay, this particular BG pioneered many formation and bombing procedures that went on to become standard operating procedures within the 8th AF. Gaining two

Below: *Flak Eater*, a B-17G, with an impressive shark's mouth insignia on its chin turret, was operated by the 364th Bomb Squadron, 305th Bomb Group, and was based at Chelveston in the late summer of 1944. (Pete West)

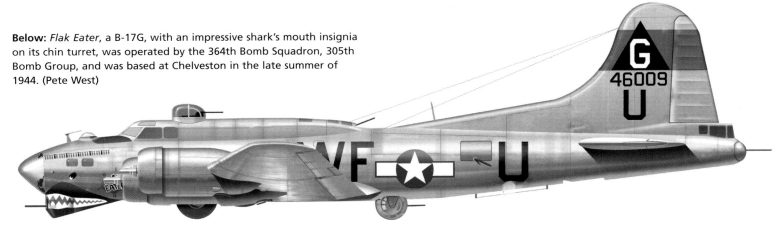

Distinguished Unit Citations and a pair of Medals of Honour during its time in the ETO, the 305th carried out its first mission on November 17, 1942, with its last on April 25, 1945, in-between which 9,231 sorties were mounted. The 422nd BS undertook the first night attack by aircraft of the 8th AF. Moving to Belgium in July 1945 the Group was thereafter employed on photo-mapping flights over Europe and North Africa.

306th Bombardment Group	
Squadrons	367th, 368th, 369th and 423rd BS
Assignment	8th AF
Models	B-17F and G
Op Period	October 1942 to May 1945
Bases	Thurleigh, UK
Losses	171 MIA

Stationed in the UK, and at one base longer than any other 8th AF Group, one of the Group's component squadrons, the 367th BS, suffered the highest losses of any unit between October 1942 and August 1943. To balance this situation, the 369th BS flew for over six months during 1943 without loss! A total of 9,614 sorties were mounted, encompassing 342 missions, during which 22,574 tons of bombs were dropped. On December 1, 1945 the 306th moved to Giebelstadt in Germany, where it carried out photo-mapping flights.

351st Bombardment Group	
Squadrons	508th, 509th, 510th and 511th BS
Assignment	8th AF
Models	B-17F and G
Op Period	May 1943 to May 1945
Bases	Polebrook, UK
Losses	124 MIA

Assigned to the 8th AF in April 1943, it served in the ETO for two years, during which time Hollywood actor Clark Gable flew a number of missions as an air gunner. It was during this period that the famed wartime documentary *Combat America* was filmed on actual raids over Germany, with Gable providing the narration for the finished production. Between June 1943 and January 1944 the 509th BS flew 54 consecutive missions without loss. After carrying out 8,600 sorties the 351st was redeployed to the USA in May and June 1945, after which it was inactivated on August 28, 1945.

Top: B-17Fs of the 366th (coded KY) and 422nd (coded JJ) Bomb Squadrons, 305th Bomb Group start making contrails in the sky on their way to bomb Lille. (US National Archives)

Above: Illustrating how the US Army Air Force's 8th Air Force operated in 'high' and 'low' formations, aircraft of the 305th Bomb Group drone their way across the sky in a mission against Villacoublay

Airfield near Paris in August 1943. In an operation that lasted over four hours, the bombers were escorted by Republic P-47 Thunderbolt fighters. (US National Archives)

Below: Mechanics give *Queenie*, a B-17G of the 527th Bomb Squadron, 379th Bomb Group, a final check over at Kimbolton, before embarking on another mission. (US National Archives)

379th Bombardment Group	
Squadrons	524th, 525th, 526th and 527th BS
Assignment	8th AF
Models	B-17F and G
Op Period	May 1943 to May 1945
Bases	Kimbolton, UK
Losses	141 MIA

A number of claims to fame distinguish this Group. *Ol Gappy*, one of its B-17s, flew an amazing 157 missions, probably more than any other in the history of the 8th AF. The 379th also had a lower abortive rate of 8th AF Groups, which saw action from 1943 onwards and it

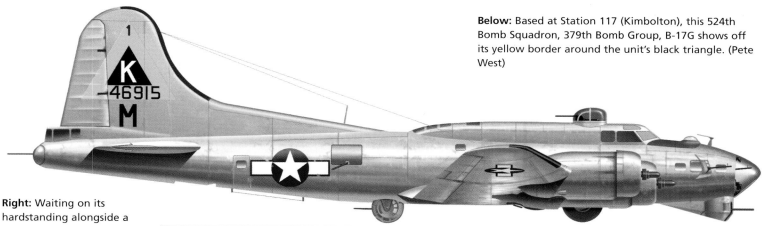

Below: Based at Station 117 (Kimbolton), this 524th Bomb Squadron, 379th Bomb Group, B-17G shows off its yellow border around the unit's black triangle. (Pete West)

Right: Waiting on its hardstanding alongside a hangar at Kimbolton in the UK ready for the next mission, B-17F 'FR-M' of the 525th Bomb Squadron, 379th Bomb Group is an inert piece of machinery. Just a few hours later it would become a living, breathing weapon of war. (US National Archives)

Right: Natural metal B-17Gs started serving with the 379th Bomb Group from March 1944. This aircraft, 42-97229, of the 524th Bomb Squadron is pictured parked on its hardstanding at Kimbolton Airfield. (Robert F Dorr)

306th BG

351st BG

379th BG

dropped a greater tonnage of bombs than any other Group – 26,459 tons in total.

381st Bombardment Group	
Squadrons	532nd, 533rd, 534th and 535th BS
Assignment	8th AF
Models	B-17F and G
Op Period	June 1943 to May 1945
Bases	Ridgewell, UK
Losses	131 MIA

Activated at Gowen Field, Idaho, USA, on November 3, 1942, the unit's ground echelon embarked for the ETO on the *Queen Elizabeth* on May 27, 1943, arriving in the UK on June 2. The air echelon started its European deployment on May 15, 1943, flying to the UK via Bangor, Gander, and making landfall at Prestwick. Suffering the

Below left: Flying Fortress of various Bomb Groups make their way out to the target. In the foreground is 42-30018, a B-17F of the 532nd Bomb Squadron, 381st Bomb Group. (US National Archives)

Below: 42-5846, *Tinker Toy*, was a B-17F operated by the 535th Bomb Squadron of the 381st Bomb Group out of Ridgewell, Essex, in autumn 1943. (Pete West)

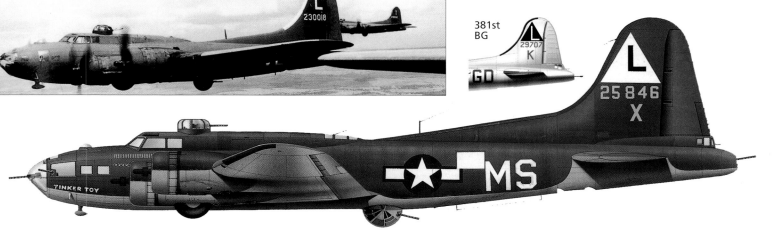

381st BG

Left: A quartet of B-17Fs from the 381st Bomb Group cruise over the patchwork quilt of English fields. (US National Archives)

388th BG

Left: All four engines are in the process of being changed on *Tomahawk Warrior*, a B-17G of the Ridgewell-based 381st Bomb Group. USAAF groundcrews endured all kinds of weather to make sure their charges were ready for action. (US National Archives)

highest losses of all 8th AF Groups on the first mission to bomb the ball-bearing works at Schweinfurt on August 17, 1943, the Group finished the war having amassed a

in June 1945 and participated in the *Green Project* operation, which comprised the moving of US forces to staging areas.

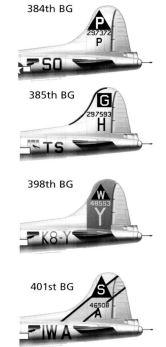

384th BG

385th BG

398th BG

401st BG

384th Bombardment Group	
Squadrons	544th, 545th, 546th and 547th BS
Assignment	8th AF
Models	B-17F and G
Op Period	June 1943 to May 1945
Bases	Grafton Underwood, UK
Losses	159 MIA

385th Bombardment Group	
Squadrons	548th, 549th, 550th and 551st BS
Assignment	8th AF
Models	B-17F and G
Op Period	July 1943 to May 1945
Bases	Great Ashfield, UK
Losses	129 MIA

total of 9,035 individual sorties, spread over 296 missions. Dropping the last 8th AF bombs of World War Two, a task it carried out on April 25, 1945, the 384th BG carried out a total of 314 missions, with 9,348 sorties to its credit before the end of hostilities. Two Distinguished Unit Citations were awarded to the Group during the course of the war, one on January 11, 1944 and the other on April 26, 1944 (the latter for participation in a raid on Oberpfafenhofen). The 384th BG moved to Istres, France,

Two of the 385th's aircraft were lost during the transit flight from the USA to the UK in May 1943. It led the famous attack on the Marienburg factory on October 9, 1943, having carried out its first ETO mission on July 17. Of its total of 296 missions, six were food-dropping sorties in Europe, in which some 184 tons of supplies were dispatched. On one of these occasions the Group's aircraft were shot on by enemy fire, thus the mission was recognised as a combat credit.

Below: Aircraft of the 545th Bomb Squadron wore 'DA' unit codes, while the black outer triangle on the tail enclosing the letter P denotes the 384th Bomb Group, which was based at Grafton Underwood. (Pete West)

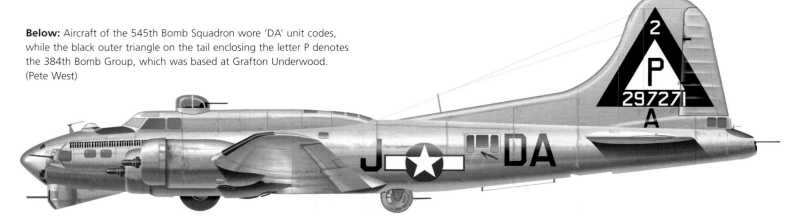

388th Bombardment Group

Squadrons	560th, 561st, 562nd and 563rd BS
Assignment	8th AF
Models	B-17F and G
Op Period	July 1943 to May 1945
Bases	Knettishall, UK
Losses	142 MIA

After completing final training at Sioux City, USA, the Group's air echelon departed for the UK in June 1943, flying the northern route, via Newfoundland, Greenland and Iceland to Prestwick, Scotland. Dropping a total of 18,163 tons of bombs, during 8,051 sorties, the unit later went on to convert to the Consolidated B-24 Liberator, after which it carried out experiments within the Aphrodite radio-controlled bomber project.

390th Bombardment Group

Squadrons	568th, 569th, 570th and 571st BS
Assignment	8th AF
Models	B-17F and G
Op Period	August 1943 to May 1945
Bases	Framlingham, UK
Losses	144 MIA

Claiming the highest number of enemy aircraft destroyed by an 8th AF bomb group during one mission (on October 10, 1943), the only man to fly 100 missions with the 8th AF, Hewitt Dunn, did so with the 390th. Awarded two Distinguished Unit Citations for operations against Regensburg and Schweinfurt in August and October respectively, the 390th BG finished the war after flying a total of 8,725 sorties, covering 300 missions.

398th Bombardment Group

Squadrons	600th, 601st, 602nd and 603rd BS
Assignment	8th AF
Models	B-17G
Op Period	May 1944 to May 1945
Bases	Nuthampstead, UK
Losses	58 MIA

This unit trained 326 B-17 crews between August and December 1943, after which it departed the USA for the UK, arriving in the spring of 1944. Staying in the ETO for just over one year, it carried out its first operational mission on May 6, 1944, with its last on April 25, 1945. A grand tally of 6,419 sorties were mounted during this period before the 398th returned to the USA in May/June 1945. It was disbanded on September 1, 1945.

401st Bombardment Group

Squadrons	612th, 613th, 614th and 615th BS
Assignment	8th AF
Models	B-17G
Op Period	November 1943 to May 1945
Bases	Deenethorpe, UK
Losses	95 MIA

Above: With the 'SC' codes denoting the 612th Bomb Squadron, the 'S' within a triangle shows that these B-17Gs are part of the Deenethorpe-based 401st Bomb Group. (US National Archives)

Below: *Bombs Away!* Aircraft of the 613th Bomb Squadron, 401st Bomb Group, let loose their deadly cargo on an enemy target during the summer of 1944. (Key Collection)

Activated at Ephrata Army Air Base, Washington, on April 1, 1943. After the unit completed its wartime training its ground echelon started to move to the ETO in October 1943, embarking on the *Queen Mary*. After final inspections at Scott Field, the air echelon left the USA bound for the UK, via Goose Bay and Iceland. The 401st was in action soon after its arrival, for on November 26 the first of a total of 7,430 wartime sorties was mounted against Germany. Gaining the second best rating for bombing accuracy in the 8th AF, the 401st brought its wartime operational service to an end on April 20, 1945, redeploying to the USA in June.

Above: Not all damage was caused by enemy action. This 401st Bomb Group B-17G has managed to venture off of the taxiway and get bogged down in the soft earth. A judicious amount of pushing and pulling soon saw it back on the straight and narrow again! (US National Archives)

447th Bombardment Group

Squadrons	708th, 709th, 710th and 711th BS
Assignment	8th AF
Models	B-17G
Op Period	December 1943 to May 1945
Bases	Rattlesden, UK
Losses	97 MIA

Flying to the UK, via the southern route in November 1943 the 447th was in action by December. Some 17,102 tons of bombs were dropped during its time in the ETO and one of its B-17s, *Milk Wagon*, set the record for a 3rd Air Division Fortress, flying 129 missions with no turn backs. After 7,605 sorties, the 447th's war came to an end, leaving Rattlesden to fly back to the USA on June 29/30, 1945, and was disbanded in the November.

452nd Bombardment Group

Squadrons	728th, 729th, 730th and 731st BS
Assignment	8th AF
Models	B-17G
Op Period	February 1944 to May 1945
Bases	Deopham Green
Losses	110 MIA

The 452nd was assigned to the 8th AF in January 1944. During the course of hostilities the Group had more Commanding Officers than any other. Despite this dubious claim to fame, the 452nd flew a total of 250 missions (including five in May 1945, to drop 369 tons of food), and amassed more than 7,000 sorties to its credit. Medals of Honor were awarded to 1st Lt Donald J Gott and 2nd Lt William E Metzger on November 9, 1944, with the entire Group receiving a Distinguished Unit Citation on April 7, 1945, for its part in an attack on Kaltenkirchen. Departing the UK for America in June 1945, the 452nd was disbanded on August 28.

457th Bombardment Group

Squadrons	748th, 749th, 750th and 751st BS
Assignment	8th AF
Models	B-17G
Op Period	February 1944 to May 1945
Bases	Glatton, UK
Losses	83 MIA

Stationed at Glatton for its entire period in the UK, the 457th completed its training programme at Ephrata Army Air Base, Washington, from late October to early December 1943, before proceeding to the ETO in January 1944. Flying its first mission on February 21, the Group completed 7,086 sorties, dropping 16,773 tons of bombs and 142 tons of leaflets before hostilities came to an end and it was time to return to the USA. It carried out the latter in late May, early June, 1945, and was disbanded by the end of August

463rd Bombardment Group

Squadrons	772nd, 773rd, 774th and 775th BS
Assignment	15th AF
Models	B-17G
Op Period	March 1944 to May 1945
Bases	Celone, Italy
Losses	100 MIA

Activated on August 1, 1943, a period of intensive training followed, after which the unit moved to Italy and

Top: *Busy Baby*, a B-17G of the 447th Bomb Group, is parked up on a rather muddy hardstanding at Rattlesden. (US National Archives)

Above: Judging by the copious exhaust stains on the undersides of the wings, *Mon Tete Rouge II*, a B-17G of the 452nd Bomb Group, has seen extensive service. (US National Archives)

Left: Heading out to the target is a mixture of camouflaged and natural metal B-17Gs of the 452nd Bomb Group. (US National Archives)

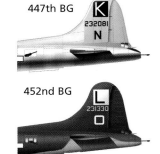

447th BG

452nd BG

457th BG

Right: This 463rd Bomb Group B-17G, 42-31684 *Joker*, is different in that it wears its name on the aircraft's fin instead of the nose, the more usual location for such markings. It also seems to have received a new rear gun turret, hence its unpainted finish. (US National Archives)

482nd BG

Bottom: Winters in Britain could be harsh! Here, the groundcrew of a B-17F warm up the engines with external hot air blowers before attempting to start the mighty radials prior to the next mission. (US National Archives)

was allocated to the 5th Bombardment Wing, based at Celone, near Foggia. It took part in the attacks against the enemy oil refineries at Ploesti, and was the only B-17 group to reach the target, due to poor weather conditions. At the end of World War Two the 463rd took part in supply missions to Prisoners of War camps in Austria. It returned to the USA and was disbanded in August 1945.

482nd Bombardment Group	
Squadrons	812th, 813th and 814th BS
Assignment	8th AF
Models	B-17F and G with radars. Also flew B-24s
Op Period	September 1943 to May 1945
Bases	Alconbury, UK
Losses	5 MIA

The only 8th AF Bomb Group to be formed and activated in the UK (Alconbury, August 20, 1943), the 482nd pioneered radar-bombing equipment (H2S, H2X and Oboe) for the USAAF. Its personnel were specially selected from 8th Bomber Command, plus men who had been involved with earlier Gee radar experiments. In a departure from normal 8th AF BGs, the 482nd had a three-fold mission: combat operations, the development of radar devices and their techniques and to train pathfinder crews. The B-17s (and later B-24s) often flew from other Groups' airfields in their capacity as lead aircraft of the mission. Between August 1944 and April 1945 the 482nd carried out 202 radar-assisted and *Nickling* (leaflet) sorties over enemy territory, without loss.

483rd Bombardment Group	
Squadrons	815th, 816th, 817th and 840th BS
Assignment	15th AF
Models	B-17G
Op Period	April 1944 to May 1945
Bases	Tortorella and Sterparone, Italy
Losses	99 MIA

Established in September 1943, the 483rd was declared operational on April 12, 1944, at Tortorella, Italy, moving

on to its permanent base at Sterparone on April 22. During an attack on Memmingen on July 18, 1944, poor weather dogged the attacking bombers, with only those from the 483rd managing to get through and bomb the target. Attacked en route by 200 enemy fighters, the unit lost 14 aircraft. This courageous action resulted in a Distinguished Unit Cross (DUC) being awarded. This was followed by another DUC as a result of the 483rd leading 15th AF aircraft on a mission to Berlin, during which concentrated numbers of Messerschmitt 262 jet fighters attacked the formation of bombers. Following the end of the war the group was disbanded on September 25, 1945.

486th Bombardment Group	
Squadrons	832nd, 833rd, 834th and 835th BS
Assignment	8th AF
Models	B-17G (Converted from B-24)
Op Period	August 1944 to May 1945
Bases	Sudbury, UK
Losses	29 MIA

Converting to the Flying Fortress from the B-24 Liberator in the ETO, its first mission with B-17s took place on August 1, 1944. Spanning some 188 missions (46 with B-24s), a total of 14,517 tons of bombs, as well as four tons of leaflets, were dropped on enemy-occupied territory. The 486th gained no major awards during its career in the UK, despite the 834th BS flying its first 78 consecutive missions with no loss to aircraft or personnel. Redeploying to the USA in early July, 1945, the Group was inactivated on November 7, 1945.

487th Bombardment Group	
Squadrons	836th, 837th 838th and 839th BS
Assignment	8th AF
Models	B-17G (Converted from B-24)
Op Period	August 1944 to May 1945
Bases	Lavenham, UK
Losses	37 MIA

On December 24, 1944, this Group led the largest 8th AF mission of World War Two, and led the 3rd Air Division in bombing accuracy from January 1945 to the end of the war. Starting life with B-24 Liberators, the 487th was initially commanded by Lt Col Beirne Lay Jr, who, after the war, went on to co-write the screenplay for the, now famous, 1949 feature film, *Twelve O'Clock High*. Flying a total of 185 missions (46 of those being with Liberators) a grand total of 14,041 tons of bombs were dropped before the unit returned to the USA in July/August 1945.

490th Bombardment Group	
Squadrons	848th, 849th, 850th and 851st BS
Assignment	8th AF
Models	B-17G (Converted from B-24)
Op Period	September 1944 to May 1945
Bases	Eye, UK
Losses	20 MIA

Another Group which started with B-24s and later converted on to the Flying Fortress, it was resident in the UK for a little over one year, before returning home for disbandment in November 1945. Claiming the lowest 'missing in action' tally of any 8th AF Bomb Group in combat for an extended period of time, the 490th notched up 158 missions, dropping more than 12,000 tons of bombs in the process.

493rd Bombardment Group	
Squadrons	860th, 861st, 862nd and 863rd BS
Assignment	8th AF
Models	B-17G (Converted from B-24)
Op Period	September 1944 to May 1945
Bases	Debach and Little Walden
Losses	30 Missing In Action (MIA)

After flying 47 missions with Liberators, the Group, which was the last in the 8th AF to become operational, changed its mount to the B-17, which it took into combat on September 8, 1944. Commanded by Col Robert B Landry, from February to May 1945, Landry was the only man to command both bomber and Fighter Groups within the 8th AF. The 493rd flew its final mission on April 20, 1945, and returned home to the USA in July and August. Like so many other combat groups, it was deactivated soon afterwards.

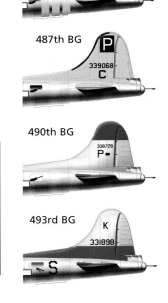

486th BG

487th BG

490th BG

493rd BG

Left: When Flying Fortresses first arrived in the European Theatre of Operations, many carried the mottled-style camouflage, as does this trio of B-17Fs. (US National Archives)

Top: The closeness to the camera of the bombs accentuates their size as they wait to be loaded aboard the B-17G. (US National Archives)

Above A typical scene on an English airfield during the summer of 1944. A mechanic watches as a B-17G takes off for an air test. (US National Archives)

Right: A Douglas C-54 Skymaster transport aircraft takes off over the line-up of B-17Gs at Marrakesh. (US National Archives)

IN GLORIOUS COLOUR

Major movie studios in Hollywood, USA, had been using colour film for a number of years before World War Two broke out (the 1939 production of *Gone With The Wind* being a classic example), but its use in wartime newsreels was limited. For instance, colour footage of Royal Air Force aircraft in action is rare, to say the least. The vast majority of surviving colour combat images are from the American forces, whose personnel seem to have enjoyed more access to non-monochrome film stock. While the vast majority of people saw the war being fought in black and white in the cinemas, we are now fortunate to be able to see the conflict from an entirely different aspect, via those well-known colour films and photographs that have survived. Another area, which should not be forgotten, is those illustrations that have emanated from private sources and archives in recent years.

Opposite page, top: B-17G Flying Fortresses of the 533rd Bomb Squadron, 381st Bomb Group, based at Ridgewell, drone over the green fields of England on their way out to bomb enemy targets. (US National Archive)

Opposite page, bottom: A relatively new-looking B-17G of the 91st Bomb Group is marshalled in by Master Sergeant Herbert H Roberts. (US National Archives)

Above: Probably posed for the cameras, Lt Col Louis Thorap and 1st Lt John Webb review their route before boarding their B-17G. (US National Archives)

Above right: This fully kitted out B-17F waist gunner ponders the next mission. Note the canvas bag attached to the gun to catch the spent cartridge cases. Later marks of Fortress had boxes mounted on the floor to fulfil this task. (US National Archives)

Right: Fins are attached to the bombs as this 'Fort' gets its final look-over by the attendant groundcrew, who are busy checking the engines and polishing the Perspex. (US National Archives)

Above: A mixture of camouflaged and natural metal B-17Gs of the 323rd Bomb Squadron, 91st Bomb Group, open their bomb doors over the target in the spring of 1944. (US National Archives)

Left: A natural metal B-17G dwarfs the squadron 'hack', Piper Cub *Pappy*. (US National Archives)

Opposite page, top: *Mary Ruth*, an olive drab-camouflaged B-17F wears the early war style American insignia on the fuselage and wings. (US National Archives)

Opposite page, centre: One can almost hear the Wright Cyclone radial engines, as these red-tailed B-17Gs of the 381st Bomb Group rumble over the patchwork fields of wartime England. Note the bomber airfield in the bottom right of the picture. (US National Archives)

Opposite page, bottom: Tight formations were flown to maximise the effectiveness of the defensive firepower. The theory was fine, but the practice often proved otherwise. B-17Gs of the 533rd Bomb Squadron, 381st Bomb Group maintain their stations. (US National Archives)

Above: This pair of B-17Fs from the 323rd Bomb Squadron, 91st Bomb Group, display the early olive drab with medium green blotching, commonplace on original combat airframes and early replacements. These colours served to give the aircraft a well-used and sometimes rundown appearance. (US National Archives)

Left: Carrying his flightbag, a crew member walks out to B-17F 42-30793, which bears the somewhat long-winded legend on the nose: *Tom Paine – Tyranny, like Hell, is not easily conquered.* (US National Archives)

GRACING THE NOSE

The application of nose art was more prevalent on American aircraft during World War Two than it ever was in the Royal Air Force. Artistic members of the air and groundcrews went to great pains to ensure that their aircraft boasted the most impressive nose art in the unit.

As a result, some highly detailed images – usually concentrating on the female form – graced the sides of numerous B-17s during the war. This was initially looked on with disdain by unit commanders, but as time went on, it became the accepted norm and there was even friendly rivalry between aircraft crews to see who could get away with the most daring images.

Nicknames almost always accompanied the illustration and these sometimes had a special significance. Quite often they would reflect popular songs of the day, *Pistol Packin Mama*, *Moonlight Serenade*, *Sleepy Time Gal* and the like, while others may have featured the name of one of the crew members, or even a blatantly provocative comment, *Mount N' Ride*, *Mis-Abortion* and *Shady Lady*.

Right: Blessed by royalty! The young Princess Elizabeth named this B-17G of the 306th Bomb Group US 8th Air Force, *Rose of York*, at Thurleigh, Beds, in July 1944. (via Imperial War Museum)

Above: Female film stars of the day often appeared on the noses of Flying Fortresses. Betty Grable, who at the height of her stardom is said to have had her legs insured for one million dollars, appears on the side of the Commemorative Air Force Arizona Wing's B-17G *Sentimental Journey*. (Key – Duncan Cubitt)

Left: One of four B-17s to carry the legend *Idiots' Delight*, Sgt Penrose Pilla puts the finishing touches to one of the bomb symbols on this aircraft of the 94th Bomb Group. (US National Archives)

Top right: The 533rd Bomb Squadron intelligence officer gets first impressions on how the sortie went from the crew as they disembark from 42-30721 *Sweet and Lovely*, one of many B-17s named after a popular song of the period. (US National Archives)

Right: *Pistol Packin Mama* was a well-known tune played by Major Glenn Miller's Band of the Allied Expeditionary Force. This B-17 of the 305th Bomb Group also features a 25-mission bomb tally above the forward fuselage windows. (US National Archives)

Above left: This Fortress earned its name *Flak Eater* after 28 missions dodging the enemy's anti-aircraft fire. The addition of a shark's mouth insignia, which encompasses the chin turret, makes the nose-art even more dramatic. (US National Archives)

Above right: A bikini-clad beauty swings on a star as the crew of 42-6174 *Woosh Woosh* poses for a group photograph. This aircraft is also thought to have carried the names *Homesick Angel* and *Stripped for Action* at other times in its 8th Air Force career. (US National Archives)

Left: Another crew shot, this time in front of a gun-toting and bomb-dropping wasp *She's a Honey*, emblazoned on the side of this 305th Bomb Group B-17G in April 1945. (US National Archives)

Opposite page, top: An incredible 100 mission symbols are chalked up on the side of *Leading Lady*, a B-17G of the 305th Bomb Group in November 1944. This aircraft later operated with the 401st BG and survived to return to the USA at the end of the war. (US National Archives)

Opposite page, bottom: *Can Do*, another B-17G of the 305th BG, featured a shattered Nazi swastika underneath a winged bomb. (US National Archives)

Far left: American groundcrew rescue a piece of nose-art, although *Stinky* is not believed to have been affixed to the B-17 fuselage in the background. (US National Archives

Near left: Another B-17F, this time *Green Mountain Rambler*, featuring a shotgun-wielding huntsman and his rather surprised-looking dog, which was operated by the 305th Bomb Group. (US National Archives)

Right: Sometimes the female form was not quite in perspective, as is the case with *Fertile Myrtle*, which graced the side of a B-17F, operated by the Bassingbourn-based 91st Bomb Group, US 8th Air Force. (Robert F Dorr)

Left: Corporal W Neville 'touches up' *Dame Satan* on the nose of B-17F 42-2990, operated by the 322nd Bomb Squadron/ 91st Bomb Group. After serving with the unit from January 1943, the Fortress was lost on the infamous Schweinfurt mission in August of the same year. (US National Archives)

Right A galloping steam-snorting stallion careers across the nose of B-17G *Man O War II – Horse-power Ltd.* Bomber artwork was often a toss-up between the ubiquitous female nude and a cartoon character. (Robert F Dorr)

THE WORLD'S SURVIVING B-17s

The numbers of airworthy examples of Boeing's most famous World War Two design are slowly increasing year by year. The task of restoring and keeping one of these four-engined bombers in the air is by no means an easy one.

None of the airworthy aircraft included in the following directory benefits from any governmental support, either monetary or in 'kind'. It is therefore down to volunteers, supporters' organisations and individuals with the required amounts of time and money to pour into the projects. Without them we would not be able to see B-17s doing what comes naturally, flying! Here we present the histories of the world's surviving flyable airframes, with an additional listing of all other existing B-17s resident in museums or undergoing restoration.

B-17F 42-29782 (N17W) *Boeing Bee*
Museum of Flight, Renton, Washington, USA

One of three surviving B-17Fs, and the sole airworthy example, 42-29782 was accepted by the US Army Air Force on February 13, 1943, and was then flown to United Airlines' modification centre at Cheyenne Airport, Wyoming, arriving there in February 17. Two weeks later it was ready for military service and was assigned to a training unit at Blythe Field, California.

Reportedly spending all of its service career with training establishments, May 1944 saw the B-17 allocated to Drew Field, Montana, where it remained until being struck of military charge in November 1945. It was then flown to the Reconstruction Finance Corporation's (RFC) facility at Altus, Oklahoma, where it was put up for disposal. At that time the RFC was in the process of making available former wartime aircraft to cities and towns that wanted to set up war memorials. As a result of this policy, 42-29782 was transferred to the city of Stuttgart, Arkansas, where it would be placed on public display. This took place in September 1946, and the B-17F ended up in a small park with the legend 'Great White Bird' emblazoned on its forward fuselage.

Five years later the local authorities had grown tired of the old bomber, which was gradually looking the worse for wear, and a deal was struck with a local individual to purchase the aircraft and remove it. In 1953 the bomber's then owner sold the Fortress on to brothers Max and John Biegeret and their business partner, Ben Widtfeldt, who were located at Lincoln, Nebraska. The team then set about restoring the veteran bomber to flying condition.

On April 21, 1954, Max Biegeret requested the allocation of a civil aircraft registration for the Fortress, asking for a number such as N17B or suchlike to reflect the aircraft's model number. As a result of what has probably got to be the first request for a 'personalised' registration for an aircraft, N17W was issued. Converted into an aerial sprayer, the B-17 was employed in a variety of different projects, clocking up a considerable number of flying hours in the process. By 1961 the aircraft had passed into the hands of Abe Sellards, one of the founders of Aviation Specialities, a company which operated a large number of B-17s in the flying tanker role during the 1960s. In 1968 and 1969 N17W became a film star when it was used in the filming of *1,000 Plane Raid* and *Tora! Tora! Tora!* respectively.

After its bout of screen stardom the Fortress continued to be employed in the spraying role, until October 1985, when it was sold to Bob Richardson, a Seattle-based businessman. In 1989 the cinema screen beckoned again,

Below: Both of the Commemorative Air Force's (CAF) B-17G Flying Fortresses, *Sentimental Journey* and *Texas Raiders*, cruise over the Texan landscape during the CAF's Airsho 99. (Key – Duncan Cubitt)

Above: Bomb-bay doors agape, *Sentimental Journey* makes a pass over Midland, Texas, during Airsho 99. (Key – Duncan Cubitt)

and N17W was flown across the Atlantic to participate in the feature film version of *Memphis Belle*. Soon after returning to the USA in late 1989, its owner died and the aircraft was incorporated into the Museum of Flight at Seattle. A thorough restoration programme was initiated, a task which was completed in 1998, and after a period of external display at Boeing Field, the bomber was flown to Renton Airport in late December 1999. It is now enjoying covered accommodation, although public access to view this, the world's oldest airworthy B-17, is not possible at the time of writing.

B-17G 44-83514 (N9323Z) *Sentimental Journey*
Commemorative Air Force, Falcon Field, Arizona, USA
The Commemorative Air Force's (CAF) B-17G *Sentimental Journey* is well known on the American airshow circuit,

having been acquired by the Arizona Wing in 1978 and restored to its original glory. The aircraft was accepted at Long Beach in March 1945 but its early history is something of a mystery. It certainly went into store but there is some suggestion that it may have made its way to the Far East and, around 1947-49 seen service with the 5th Reconnaissance Group out of Clark Field, Philippines as an RB-17G. It re-appeared at Olmsted in 1950 and was subsequently converted to drone standard and probably served with the 3205th Drone Group. By 1956 it was with the 3215th Drone Squadron at Patrick AFB. The aircraft retired to Davis-Monthan in mid-1959 but in July of that year was sold at auction for $5,289 and registered as N9323Z. It was sold on to Western Air Industries at Anderson, California, for conversion to a fire-bomber. It served in this role until

	Civil				
Mark	**Identity**	**Registration**	**Name**	**Operator/Location**	**Country**
B-17F	42-29782	N17W	*Boeing Bee*	Museum of Flight, Renton, WA	USA
B-17G	44-83514	N9323Z	*Sentimental Journey*	CAF, Falcon Field, AX	USA
B-17G	44-83546	N3703G	Memphis Belle	MARC, Farmingdale, NY	USA
B-17G	44-83563	N9563Z	*Fuddy Duddy*	NWM, Horseheads, NY	USA
B-17G	44-83575	N93012	*Nine O Nine*	Collings Foundation, Stow, MA	USA
B-17G	44-83785	N207EV	—	Evergreen Vintage Aircraft Inc, Portland, OR	USA
B-17G	44-83872	N7227C	*Texas Raiders*	CAF Gulf Coast Wing, Houston, TX	USA
B-17G	44-85718	N900RW	*Thunderbird*	Lone Star Flight Museum, Galveston, TX	USA
B-17G	44-85740	N5017N	*Aluminium Overcast*	EAA, Oshkosh, WI	USA
B-17G	44-85778	N3509G	*Miss Angela*	Palm Springs Air Museum, CA	USA
B-17G	44-485784	G-BEDF	*Sally B*	B-17 Preservation, Duxford, Cambs	UK
B-17G	44-85829	N3193G	*Yankee Lady*	Yankee Air Force, Ypsilanti, MI	USA
B-17G	44-8543	N3701G	*Chuckie*	Vintage Flying Machines, Fort Worth, TX	USA
B-17G	44-8846	F-AZDX	*Pink Lady*	Fortresse Toujours Volante, Paris	France

B-17 SURVIVORS DIRECTORY – AIRWORTHY AIRCRAFT

After being known as the Confederate Air Force since its founding in 1957, the CAF changed its operating name to Commemorative Air Force on January 1, 2002. This book however contains a number of references to the CAF, the majority of which relate to the time when the organisation was still 'Confederate'.

1977 and was then put up for disposal, along with the rest of Aero Union's B-17 fleet. It was then acquired by the Arizona CAF. Since then many thousands of man-hours, along with a considerable amount of money, has been expended in getting this aircraft back into stock military configuration. In 1978, it made a brief static appearance in Steven Spielberg's cinema film *1941*, since when it has made a number of airshow appearances each year, clocking up an ever-increasing number of flying hours. Now well in excess of 7,000 hours, and with an average of 150 hours amounted each year, it is a mammoth task keeping this bomber in the air. Donations and airshow expenses help the cause, but the bulk of the work and funding is undertaken by the dedicated members of the CAF's Arizona Wing, all fiercely proud of their charge.

B-17G 44-83546 (N3703G) *Memphis Belle*

Military Aircraft Restoration Corp, Farmingdale, New York, USA

Converted to CB-17G configuration after it was delivered to the Army Air Force in 1945, it was subsequently assigned to the Air Transport Command and flown to San Francisco, California. After passing through a number of different units it was redesignated as a VB-17G in October 1948 and was transferred to the Strategic Air Command, serving at Andrews AFB and Offut AFB. During the Korean War it joined the Far East Air Force and while based in Japan flew operationally as well as being used as the personal transport of Major General Glenn Barcus.

After the Korean War came to an end, 44-83546 was flown to Davis-Monthan AFB, where it was put into storage. It remained there until April 1949 when it was offered for disposal. Sold at auction for $2,686 it was purchased by the National Metals Company of Phoenix, Arizona. Just six weeks later it was sold again, this time to Fastway Air Inc at Long Beach, California. Fastway converted the bomber for fire-fighting duties, it being one of the first B-17s to be reconfigured for this purpose.

After seeing considerable service in the fire suppressant role, age eventually caught up with N3703G and it was sold during the late 1970s to David Tallichet's Military Aircraft Restoration Corp (MARC). Initially based at Long Beach, the collection moved to Chino Airport, California, and work commenced to put the Fortress back into World War Two configuration. Repainted in the colours of a B-17F, gun turrets and other operational internal equipment was fitted to bring the aircraft up to military specification.

Contracted for use in the filming of *Memphis Belle* in spring 1989, the Fortress flew the Atlantic to the UK, where cosmetic work was carried out to complete the transformation from B-17G to B-17F model. Flying some 50 hours for the filming, the B-17 departed the UK in August 1989, its film assignment having come to an end. Upon return to the USA the bomber was put on display at March Field Museum, although it also continued to participate at airshows. During 2000 the Fortress took up residence at the American Airpower Museum, located at the former Republic Aircraft Company factory at Farmingdale, New York. It still wears its *Memphis Belle* film markings.

7

Opposite page top: Actress Betty Grable, star of such Hollywood films as *Million Dollar Legs* and *Pin-Up Girl*, adorns the nose of the CAF's B-17G 44-83514 (N9323Z). (Key – Duncan Cubitt)

Opposite page centre: One of two American-based Fortresses, which flew to the UK in 1989 for the filming of *Memphis Belle*, MARC's B-17F is pictured at Duxford receiving its movie markings. (Key – Duncan Cubitt)

Opposite page bottom: A member of the film company's art department gives the B-17 its *Memphis Belle* nose art. (Key – Duncan Cubitt)

Right: Nose-art on B-17G *Fuddy Duddy* resembles a shotgun-carrying *Elmer Fudd* cartoon character. (Key – Duncan Cubitt)

Below: Lifting off from the grass runway at Geneseo, New York, in 1990, *Fuddy Duddy* gets airborne for its display slot. (Key – Duncan Cubitt)

B-17G 44-83563 (N9563Z) Fuddy Duddy

National Warplane Museum, Horseheads, New York, USA/American Airpower Museum, Farmingdale, New York, USA

This Flying Fortress was put into storage immediately after its acceptance by the USAAF on April 7, 1945. Just a month later it was redesignated as a CB-17 and emerged as a staff transport. Flown by the Far East Air Force's Pacific Air Services Command, based in Japan, there is evidence that it was used to transport General Dwight D Eisenhower on at least one occasion. It returned to the USA in February 1952 and after a complete overhaul returned to Japan for use with the 6003rd Base Flight Squadron of the 6000th Base Service Group, based at Haneda.

Its useful life over, the B-17 returned to the USA in June 1955 and was put into storage at Davis-Monthan AFB. Remaining in situ for three years, it was put up for disposal in 1958, being purchased by the American

Compressed Steel Corporation (ACSC) at Cincinnati, Ohio. ACSC was in the business of supplying former military aircraft to civilian and foreign customers and soon sold N9563Z, plus two other Fortresses, to Aero-American, an organisation led by Greg Board.

In 1960, B-17s were being sought by John Crewdson of the UK-based Film Aviation Services, for use in a forthcoming cinema film, *The War Lover*. Purchased by Crewdson, N9563Z was joined by a pair of former US Navy PB-1Ws (N5229V and N5232V) from Dallas and the three aircraft were prepared for the long ferry flight to the UK.

Given a coat of wartime camouflage and the requisite number of gun turrets, the three Fortresses excelled in their starring roles. Much of the filming took place at RAF Bovingdon, Herts, including a stunning low-level flypast by one of the Fortresses, carried out by Crewdson himself. At the end of 'shooting' only one B-17, N9563Z, returned

to the USA. Sadly the other pair were broken up to escape import duties.

After some film promotional work the B-17 was sold again, this time to Aviation Specialities of Phoenix, Arizona, and embarked on a new career as an aerial fire-fighter. It was during this period that the silver screen beckoned again, as Aviation Specialities provided five Flying Fortresses for use in the 1970 film *Tora! Tora! Tora!*. In October 1985, the B-17 was put up for auction and was acquired, for a reported $250,000, by the National Warplane Museum (NWM), which was then located at Geneseo, New York. After flying in bare metal for a couple of years the NWM painted the aircraft to represent *Fuddy Duddy*, a Fortress of the 447th Bomb Group. As this book closed for press it had been reported that the National Warplane Museum, operators of the B-17 for some 17 years, had put *Fuddy Duddy* up for sale and that the Farmingdale-based American Airpower Museum was one of the interested parties.

B-17G 44-83575 (N93012) *Nine O Nine*
Collings Foundation, Stow, Massachusetts, USA

One of seven B-17s used to assess the vulnerability of parked aircraft to atomic bombs, 44-83575 has, in more ways than one, led a charmed life. Rolling off the Douglas production line on April 7, 1945, the bomber spent time at the Tulsa and Cheyenne modification centres before it was ready for military service on May 18. This aircraft's operational career is shrouded in mystery but it is thought that, at some time, it was deployed to the Caribbean and possibly South Africa.

Redesignated as a TB-17H it was allocated to the 1st Air Sea Rescue Squadron, complete with underslung lifeboat, but in 1952 was transferred to the Special Weapons Centre at Kirkland AFB in February 1952. Thought never to have actually been based at Kirkland, it moved on to the Air Force Special Weapons Command, where its future would take a totally different direction as it, along with another six Fortresses, was flown to the Yucca Flats, Nevada, part of the Atomic Energy Commission's test site. Beginning in 1951, this location became the location for the US government's domestic nuclear testing.

Parked at various distances from the actual detonations, the B-17s, along with other types, were used to assess the effects of atomic weapons on aircraft airframes. They were subjected to three detonations in 1952, as part of Operation *Snapper*. After evaluating the damage caused, the final report concluded that aircraft designs similar to the B-17 were most vulnerable to nuclear explosions. At the completion of the tests the various aircraft were towed to the edge of the facility and left to 'cool off'. In 1964, then deemed to be safe, the B-17, along with a host of other aircraft and parts, was put up for sale.

Purchased for the princely sum of $269 by Valley Scrap Metal, it was almost immediately resold to Aircraft Specialities, which was given just six weeks to remove it from the site. A mass of work was carried out on the bomber and despite the odds it was ready to fly by the end of the allotted period. Now named *Lady Yucca* it departed for Falcon Field, Mesa, Arizona, on May 14, 1965. Further restoration work took another ten years to complete before the B-17 was ready to join Aircraft Specialities' tanker fleet.

In October 1985, N93012 was sold to warbird collector Bob Collings and in January 1987 was ferried to Tom Reilly's rebuild facility at Kissimmee, Florida, for a complete overhaul. It was decided to finish the Fortress in the markings of *Nine O Nine*, an aircraft of the 91st Bomb Group, US 8th Air Force, which had a particularly distinguished war record, having flown 140 missions without having to abort for any reason, mechanical or weather.

Emerging from Reilly's workshops in fine fettle at the end of July 1987, the B-17 soon started to make appearances on the airshow circuit. Sadly, just one month later, during an airshow at Beaver County Airport, Pennsylvania, the Fortress suffered major damage when it ran off the end of the runway and down a 100ft (30.4m) embankment. The damage incurred by the aircraft would have normally deemed it a write-off, but for the dedication of Bob Collings, who arranged for the bomber to be transported to a hangar where repairs could be carried out.

A mass of work then took place, which entailed removal of the wings, repairs to the engines and engine nacelles, overhauling the propellers, much sheet metal work and the fitting of replica dorsal and ball gun turrets. Amazingly *Nine O Nine* was back in airworthy condition in time for the 1990 display season.

B-17G 44-83785 (N207EV)
Evergreen Vintage Aircraft Inc, Portland, Oregon, USA

This B-17 has a most confusing history, as at some stage in its career its identity was confused with that of 44-85531, an aircraft which at one time served with America's Central Intelligence Agency (CIA). The aircraft's present records show that 44-83785 was built by Douglas at Long Beach, California, and was accepted by the USAAF on June 22, 1945.

After modifications it was issued to the Hawaiian Air Wing and served at Hickam AFB as a CB-17G, with the Pacific Air Command's 1500th Military Supply Group. Moving to Haneda, Japan, for the Far East Air Force in September 1949, it spent much of the following five years with the 6101st Base Wing at Komaki. Its military records come to a close in December 1956 and it is here that the bomber's identity becomes shrouded in mystery. At some time its records become mixed with 44-85531, which, during this period was operated as N809Z initially by Atlantic-General Enterprises, of Washington, and subsequently by Intermountain Aviation. It is believed that it was then used by the CIA for delivering secret agents, photo reconnaissance and a range of other covert activities. Its external identity is reported to have been altered on several occasions to confuse those who were trying to keep track of the B-17's movements, while all internal identification plates were removed in case the aircraft fell into 'enemy' hands.

Initially registered with the Federal Aviation Administration (FAA) as 44-85531 (N809Z), further documentation suggested that the aircraft was actually 44-83785, and the records were duly amended by the FAA in May 1961. The following year the B-17 was modified to carry a boom attached to the nose section, at the end of which was a 'Y'-shaped arrangement, which became known as the 'Skyhook' system. This was

supposedly so that firefighters could be scooped up on the end of a line, which the B-17 would pick up. It is not known whether this system was actually put to serious use, although a good example of the logic behind it came when N809Z was loaned to Eon Productions/United Artists to supposedly scoop up special agent James Bond 007 at the end of the 1965 film *Thunderball*.

During the 1970s the B-17 was used in the fire-bombing role until Intermountain Aviation and its assets were transferred to the ownership of Evergreen Helicopters of McMinnville, Oregon. Its civil registration was changed to N207EV on March 6, 1979, and restoration to standard configuration began in 1985.

Much work has since taken place on the veteran aircraft, which is now adorned with the markings of the 490th Bomb Group, USAAF, representing an aircraft which operated in the UK during World War Two as part of the famed 8th Air Force.

Left: *Texas Raiders*, the CAF Gulf Coast Wing's Houston-based B-17G, is a regular participant in the impressive *Tora! Tora! Tora!* attack on Pearl Harbor routine. (Key – Duncan Cubitt)

Below left: With a smoking gun and confederate flags, a Texan cowgirl perches atop a bomb on the nose of 44-83872 (N7227C). Note the two camera symbols on the chin turret fairing. (Key – Duncan Cubitt)

B-17G 44-83872 (N7227C) *Texas Raiders*

Commemorative Air Force Gulf Coast Wing, Houston, Texas, USA

The Commemorative Air Force's (CAF) *Texas Raiders* was one of the first B-17 warbirds, having been acquired by the CAF in September 1967. The aircraft was accepted by the USAAF in July 1945 and transferred to the Navy to become a PB-1W. It remained at NAS Johnsville until May 1947 when it moved to NAS Quonset Point to serve with VX-4 as '77235.

It served with VX-4 and VW-2 at various locations for seven years, including a period of test work to evaluate an Airborne Moving Target Indicator System, during which time it was based back at NAS Johnsville. In 1954, after overhaul at NAS Norfolk and NAS San Diego it was assigned to the West Coast Early Warning Squadron and based at Atsugi, Japan, with VW-1.

Retired from the US Navy in July 1955, it was struck off the inventory just under a year later and put up for sale with a number of other PB-1Ws. Aero Services Corporation (ASC) acquired the Fortress in October 1957. It was given the civil registration N7227C and flown to Philadelphia, where it was converted to carry a high altitude magnetometer. This was the start of a period in which the B-17 would be extensively modified to carry a whole host of experimental equipment.

In 1963, it flew to northern Canada with two tons of equipment on board, which enabled a thorough survey of the solar eclipse to be carried out. However, its days as a working aircraft were numbered, for in 1965 it was used as a high-profile backdrop at the retirement ceremony for General Curtis LeMay. For this event its civil paint scheme was adorned with the markings of the 305th Bomb Group. Preservation as a warbird then beckoned with the Confederate Air Force becoming interested in acquiring the airframe. The CAF was, at that time, starting to collect bombers to add to its fleet of World War Two fighters, and N7227C, after some negotiation, joined the ranks of the then relatively new organisation, based at Mercedes, Texas.

Until the CAF came on the scene, nobody had attempted to privately operate an aircraft as large as the B-17 and initially it was flown in its civilian configuration, still wearing its ASC paint scheme, but with the addition of a number of Confederate rebel flags. As time progressed the CAF decided to put its aircraft into period military markings and the B-17 was duly painted in full 305th BG colours, with the serial 41-24592 on the tail. Later, gun turrets and other military equipment was added, but it was not until 1983, when the bomber was transferred to the CAF's Gulf Coast Wing, at Houston, Texas, that an in-depth restoration programme was initiated.

Rolled out of the Gulf Coast's hangar in June 1986, the Fortress was resplendent in accurate colours representing an aircraft of the 533rd Bomb Squadron, 381st BG. One of the longest-active warbirds in the USA, *Texas Raiders* can often be seen in company with the CAF's Liberator as the two grand old ladies tour the USA on promotional and airshow appearances.

B-17G 44-85718 (N900RW) *Thunderbird*

Lone Star Flight Museum, Galveston, Texas, USA

This former French-based Institut Geographique National (IGN) Fortress was one of 14 of the type operated for aerial survey work by the company during the post-war years. Remaining operational until 1984, when it flew to the UK to join a warbird collection, it now resides in fine fettle with the Lone Star Flight Museum at Galveston, Texas, and is seen on a regular basis at air events throughout the USA.

Seeing no military operational service whatsoever, 44-85718 spent all of its time in modification and storage facilities after being accepted by the USAAF in 1945. In October 1945, it was declared as surplus to requirements and flown to Altus, Oklahoma, remaining there for two years before being acquired, along with three other B-17s, by IGN. Ferried to France as F-BEEC and overhauled at Villacoublay, the Fortress was modified for the photo-mapping role and was later used for magnetometer survey work.

Below: Parked on the grass at Oshkosh in 1997, *Thunderbird* is the jewel in the Lone Star Flight Museum's crown. (Key – Duncan Cubitt)

The IGN B-17s were flown around the world over the next 30 years, with F-BEEC taking up the South African registration of ZS-EEC between August 1965 and August the following year. Of the total 14 purchased by IGN, by the time of 'EEC's retirement in 1984, seven B-17s remained. Of these, six have been preserved throughout Europe and the USA.

Sold to UK warbird collector, Doug Arnold, in 1984, F-BEEC was given the appropriate registration G-FORT and flown to Blackbushe, home of Arnold's Warbirds of Great Britain collection. It was later sold to Stephen Grey of The Fighter Collection, Duxford, and was ferried across to the former Battle of Britain fighter station, where it underwent some engineering work, prior to being sold on to USA resident Robert Waltrip and re-registered as N900RW in June 1987.

Before the bomber departed the UK it was painted in markings which represented *Thunderbird*, an aircraft of the 303rd Bomb Group. It left Duxford on July 14, 1987, and arrived at Houston two days later. It was immediately rolled into the Lone Star Flight Museum's maintenance workshop where a complete restoration was embarked upon. The bomber was found to be in overall good condition, with little corrosion in the airframe. Previous modifications had been carried out with a modicum of disruption to the structure, which augured well for a speedy conclusion to the work required. During the rebuild a full complement of gun turrets was added to the B-17, all military systems, bomb-bay doors etc were made operable and the Fortress eventually emerged in superb condition after a good deal of money and many man-hours had been spent on its re-birth.

Appearing at airshows throughout the USA, the B-17 is often a participant at the Experimental Aircraft Association's annual convention at Oshkosh, Wisconsin.

B-17G 44-85740 (N5017N) *Aluminium Overcast*
Experimental Aircraft Association, Oshkosh, Wisconsin, USA

With its military career consisting of just ferry flights from storage facilities to modification centres, this Fortress was delivered to Altus, Oklahoma and declared as surplus to requirements on November 7, 1945, just seven months after being accepted by the USAAF at Lockheed's Burbank factory. Purchased 18 months later for the princely sum of $750 by the Metal Products company of Amarillo, Texas, it was rapidly sold for $1,000 to Universal Aviation of Tulsa, Oklahoma, an aerial survey company, which registered it as N5017N. This was the first civilian organisation to use the Flying Fortress in a commercial role.

In August 1947, it changed ownership again and passed into the hands of Charles Winters at Miami, Florida, who intended using the B-17 for a Caribbean cargo airline venture. However, this was not to be, as just two weeks later the Fortress was sold again. This time the Vero Beach Export and Import Company became the owners of the aircraft. Modified for air cargo operations, the B-17, still with only 37 flying hours on the airframe from new, entered service and carried a consignment of beef from Florida to Puerto Rico.

Two years later it was sold, yet again, this time for $28,000, to Aero Service Corporation of Philadelphia and moved to Trenton, New Jersey, where it was fitted out for high altitude mapping flights. Operating in the Middle East, it returned to the USA for a major overhaul in May 1953, after which it returned to the Middle East and was extensively flown from Libya over the following three years, clocking up 3,325 hours flying time.

In 1962, the B-17 was sold to a company at Coatsville, Pennsylvania, which intended to convert it for spraying. This didn't happen and it was sold again in 1966 to

Above: With 'three greens' on the undercarriage selector and 'full flap', the EAA's Fortress sets up for a landing at Oshkosh in 1995. (Key – Duncan Cubitt)

Above: Pictured minus its chin gun turret at Minneapolis in 1995, Bob Pond's B-17G *Miss Angela* is currently based at the Planes of Fame Museum's Palm Springs facility. (Key – Duncan Cubitt)

Dothan Aviation of Alabama. Under contract to the American Department of Agriculture, the Fortress was fitted with a hopper and the requisite spray bars and was used by a number of state agencies against the fire ant. By 1976, the spray contract had come to an end and the B-17 was on the move again, this time to a private individual, William Harrison of Tulsa, Oklahoma, who was putting together plans to fly the Fortress around the world.

With its ownership transferred to B-17 Around The World Inc, the Fortress was prepared for its epic flight. Given a coat of combat markings, with the legend *Aluminium Overcast* on the nose, but retaining the bulk of its civilian modifications, it soon however became apparent that the sheer cost and logistics of mounting such a flight were beyond the capabilities of Harrison and his associates. The B-17 was subsequently donated to the Experimental Aircraft Association (EAA) at Oshkosh, Wisconsin, in March 1981.

After making a number of appearances at airshows it was decided to ground the bomber and put it on display in the EAA's Eagle Hangar museum building. Over the years a restoration programme has been implemented, including a full repaint in wartime markings representing an aircraft of the 601st Bomb Squadron, 398th Bomb Group. Two gun turrets have been fitted and when funding permits, original internal equipment is being refitted. In recent years the Fortress has taken to the air again, making a limited number of appearances, mainly at the annual EAA Convention.

B-17G 44-85778 (N3509G) *Miss Angela*
Palm Springs Air Museum, California, USA

Currently operated by Bob Pond's Planes of Fame organisation, this B-17 was built at Burbank and delivered to the USAAF in June 1945. After a number of

service modifications had been carried out on the airframe it was put straight into storage, until finally being delivered to the 4112th Base Unit at Olmstead in February 1946.

One month later, it was allocated to Caribbean Air Command as a TB-17G and flew to Borinquin Field, Puerto Rico, to join the 24th Composite Group. June 1948 saw the fortress move to Rio de Janeiro for the Brazilian Military Command. Two years later, still on the strength of this unit, it was redesignated as a VB-17G. Its final two years with the military were spent at Boling AFB, Washington, after which it was retired and put into storage at Davis-Monthan. Put up for disposal in August 1959, it was sold for $2,888, to Ace Smelting, which registered it as N3509G, and promptly sold it on to Sonora Flying Service at Columbia, California. It only remained with this company for 12 months before being sold again, this time to Leo Demers in Oregon.

The Fortress then took the standard post-war route for its type and was converted to become a tanker aircraft. Aero Union acquired the B-17, as Tanker 16, in April 1966. Subsequent exchanges – to Tanker 42 with Central Air Services in June 1972, and Tanker 102 with Western Aviation Contractors in July 1978 – brought the aircraft to the end of its fire-fighting career. It moved to Mojave, California, after being sold on to Aircraft Component Equipment Services, in May 1982. It then went through a succession of private owners, finally ending up in the ownership of warbird collector Bob Pond. Initially painted up as *Miss Museum of Flying*, it moved to Pond's Planes of Fame East Museum at Flying Cloud Airport, Minneapolis, Minnesota, and was subsequently renamed as *Miss Angela*. After a number of years at Flying Cloud, Pond closed the facility down and moved his collection to Palm Springs, California, in the mid 1990s, where the Fortress still resides today.

B-17G 44-85784 (G-BEDF) *Sally B*

B-17 Preservation Ltd, Duxford, Cambs UK

Without doubt the most famous of the B-17s preserved in Europe, *Sally B* is kept in airworthy condition due to the determination of a small band of pilots, engineers and volunteers. Since 1975, they have lavished the requisite amount of tender loving care needed to keep this wartime aviation icon up in the skies, where she belongs!

Accepted by the USAAF at Burbank, California, on June 19, 1945, the Fortress was assigned, after modification, to Wright Field, Ohio, where it was employed in a number of test programmes, even to the extent of having man-carrying pods fitted to the wingtips. By September 1950, it was carrying out development work for infra-red tracking systems and was based at Schenectady, New York. After its withdrawal from service, the B-17 was transferred to Olmstead AFB where it was offered for disposal. Purchased by the France-based Institut Geographique National, and allocated the civilian registration F-BGSR, it flew to its new European home in

Top: The Yankee Air Force's B-17G is in pristine condition, its polished natural metal skin positively gleaming in the American sunshine. (Key – Duncan Cubitt)

Above: Preserving her modesty, with the strategic use of 'Uncle Sam's' hat, the *Yankee Lady* adopts a typical pose on the nose of 44-85829 (N3193G). (Key – Duncan Cubitt)

preservation movement. Starring roles in television, in *We'll Meet Again*, and film, in *Memphis Belle*, have kept the aircraft in the public eye. Help to keep the B-17 airworthy comes in all shapes and sizes, and from all directions, not least from the *Sally B* Supporters' Club.

The aircraft suffered a number of expensive engine failures during 1998, which effectively grounded the Fortress. The B-17 Charitable Trust was formed in January 2000 to help raise the funding required to keep the B-17 airworthy. *Sally B* appeared at the 2000 Mildenhall Air Fete and went on to make a limited number of display appearances during the year. It is hoped that financial support will be forthcoming to maintain the aircraft in an airworthy condition for many years to come.

B-17G 44-85829 (N3193G) *Yankee Lady*

Yankee Air Force, Ypsilanti, Michigan, USA

One of the latest B-17s to be restored to flying condition, *Yankee Lady*, is a fine example of the restorer's art. One of 15 Vega-built Fortresses used by the US Coast Guard for air-sea rescue duties as PB-1Gs, 44-85829 was kept busy, flying from Newfoundland, North Carolina and California, until its retirement from active service in 1959.

Sold to the Ace Smelting Company for $5,887 in May 1959, and registered as N3193G, the aircraft was reportedly flown to Arizona. By November, it had been sold on to Fairchild Aerial Survey of Los Angeles, California, who reworked the airframe to carry aerial survey equipment. Five years later the Fortress was on the move again, this time to the Aero Service Corporation of Philadelphia, who only kept the aircraft for three months before selling it.

By 1966, the B-17 was being flown by Aircraft Specialities, who operated one of the largest fleets of Flying Fortress air tankers. In 1969, the aircraft enjoyed a brief glimpse of film stardom, when it was used with four

October 1954. Operated on high-level survey flights, the Fortress was fitted with various radar systems, infra-red sensors and photo equipment to aid it in its task. Its new occupation took the B-17 all over the world, until it was retired from active use in 1970. Five years later 44-485784 was acquired by UK-based businessman Ted White, who, along with his American colleague, Duane Egli, had the aircraft transferred to the US civil register as N17TE, before flying it to Biggin Hill Airport, Kent, UK.

The bomber soon became a worthy addition to the ranks of privately operated warbirds in the UK and made numerous airshow appearances, initially in the hands of Don Bullock and subsequently Keith Sissons. After Ted White's untimely death in 1982 B-17 Preservation Ltd was set up to operate the aircraft in the UK. Led by a human dynamo, in the shape of Elly Sallingboe, B-17 Preservation has kept this large aircraft in the forefront of the British

other B-17s, during the making of *Tora! Tora! Tora!*. Returning to its tanker task, the aircraft soldiered on until the Yankee Air Force (YAF) acquired it in 1986 for $250,000, thanks to major financial support from former 381st BG veteran Joe Slavik (hence the bomber's current colour scheme).

Ferried to the YAF's headquarters at Ypsilanti, Michigan, it was immediately grounded so that a major restoration could take place of the airframe and its systems. The whole programme took nine years to complete, with more than 300 volunteers becoming involved at various stages of the rebuild. Flying for the first time after restoration on July 13, 1995, a number of test and check-out flights took place before the B-17 made its first public appearance at the EAA's Convention at Oshkosh later that month.

Flying in a highly polished natural metal colour scheme, adorned with the markings of the 534th Bomb Squadron, 381st Bomb Group, *Yankee Lady* is one of a few such aircraft that the US Federal Aviation Administration has licensed to carry out flight experience rides. Funding from this goes towards keeping the bomber in airworthy condition.

B-17G 44-8543 (N3701G) *Chuckie*

Vintage Flying Machines, Fort Worth, Texas, USA

It is thought that this Fortress may have a wartime combat record, but so far documentary evidence has been difficult to ascertain whether this is correct. It is, however, one of the few individually-owned B-17s in the world today, being operated by Dr William and Chuckie Hospers of Fort Worth, Texas.

A Vega-built aircraft, it was accepted by the US military in October 1944, but its confirmed records only really start towards the end of 1945, by which time it was a TB-17G and was based at Patterson Field, Ohio. During the late 1940s the aircraft served with the All Weather Flying Centre at Clinton Field, Ohio, after

which it flew with the Wright Air Development Centre at Wright-Patterson (W-P) AFB. Staying at W-P until November 1952, it was then operated under contract to the Federal Telecommunications Corporation and was fitted with wingtip antennas and experimental electronic equipment. By March 1959, it was in storage at Davis-Monthan AFB and was made available for sale in May.

The same year it was bought for $5,000 by the American Pressed Steel Company and registered as N3701G. Purchased with two other B-17s, the bomber was flown to Ryan Field, Tucson, under the auspices of Aero-Associates, but by 1961 all three were advertised for sale. After a short period in the employ of the Albany Building Corporation of Fort Lauderdale, Florida, when the aircraft was used to transport vegetables, it passed into the hands of Dothan Aviation in 1963. Aerial tanker duties beckoned and for the next 13 years it battled fire ants for the Department of Agriculture in Georgia and Florida.

On October 4, 1979, the B-17 was sold to Doctor William Hospers, who had been on the lookout for an available Flying Fortress for some time. This was a giant leap for William – to actually own his own B-17 instead of continuing to admire them from afar. With a dedicated band of volunteers the bomber was slowly put back into its wartime configuration, with gun turrets and internal equipment progressively being added. A military colour scheme was applied, that of the 486th Bomb Group, which it is thought the aircraft served with during World War Two.

William's wife, Chuckie, was the driving force behind the setting up of the 'B-17 Co-op', an organisation which has brought together the owners of Fortresses throughout the world, with the aim of pooling resources in the search for parts and consumables. Lovingly looked after by the Hospers and their supporters, *Chuckie* averages about 50 flying hours each year and can be seen attending a number of air events in the USA.

Above: Captured on film at Harlingen in 1983, *Chuckie* is owned and operated by Texas-based Doctor William Hospers and his wife, Chuckie, hence the aircraft's name! (Key – Duncan Cubitt)

Above right: In its early years of preservation FTV's B-17 carried the name *Lucky Lady* and is seen here landing at the 1985 Great Warbirds Air Display, staged at West Malling, Kent. (Key – Duncan Cubitt)

Right: Now painted as *Pink Lady*, the French-based Fortress is a regular performer at airshows throughout Europe. (Key – Duncan Cubitt)

B-17G 44-8846 (F-AZDX) *Pink Lady*

Fortresse Toujours Volante, Paris, France

With a proven war record, 44-8846 is the only 'blooded' B-17 to remain in airworthy condition outside the USA. Taken on charge by the USAAF on January 13, 1945, and after passing through the modification centre at Cheyenne, Wyoming, it was flown across the Atlantic for service with the 8th Air Force in the UK. Operating with the 305th and 351st Bomb Groups for the final months of World War Two, the Fortress remained in Europe at the end of hostilities as part of the occupying forces' inventory.

By 1949, it had been redesignated as an RB-17G and flew out of Wiesbaden in Germany. Ending its military career with the 7499th Composite Squadron, it was transferred to the French-based IGN, who registered it as F-BGSP, and spent the following 30 years based at Creil.

Used for high-level survey and research tasks, *Sierra Papa* was eventually retired from active use in the early 1980s, but continued to fly on an infrequent basis in a semi-restored condition, carrying 381st BG markings, with the legend *Lucky Lady* on the nose. The continued operation of the Fortress was regularised when a consortium of sponsors, Fortresse Toujours Volante, came forward to support the aircraft.

Taking part in the filming of the 1980 movie *Memphis Belle*, the B-17 operated out of Duxford and Binbrook in the UK. Upon its return to Paris it continued to fly in the film colour scheme, until given a complete repaint in the markings of the 511th Bomb Squadron, 351st BG, US 8th Air Force. A regular participant at air events in Europe and the UK, *Pink Lady* is the last of the IGN B-17s to remain airworthy in France.

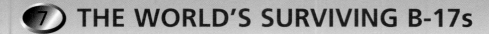

B-17 SURVIVORS DIRECTORY – AIRCRAFT PRESERVED: STORED OR UNDER RESTORATION				
Mark	**Identity**	**Name**	**Owner/Location**	**Country**
B-17D	40-3097*	The Swoose	National Air & Space Museum, Suitland, MD	USA
B-17E	41-2595*	—	Galt Airport, Marengo, IL	USA
B-17E	41-9032*	My Gal Sal	Bob Ready, Blue Ash Airport, Cincinatti, OH	USA
B-17E	41-9210*	—	Flying Heritage Collection, Arlington, WA	USA
B-17F	41-24485+	Memphis Belle	Mud Island, Memphis, TN	USA
B-17F	42-3374+	—	USAF Museum, Offut AFB, Omaha, NE	USA
B-17G	42-32076+	Shoo Shoo Shoo Baby	USAF Museum, Dayton, OH	USA
B-17G	43-38636+	*Virgin's Delight*	Castle Air Museum, Atwater, CA	USA
B-17G	44-6393+	—	March Field Museum, Riverside, CA	USA
B-17G	44-8889*	—	Musée de l'Air, Paris	France
B-17G	44-83512+	Heaven's Above	USAF History Museum, Lackland AFB, San Antonio, TX	USA
B-17G	44-83525*	—	Weeks Air Museum, Kissimmee, FL	USA
B-17G	44-83542*	Susy Q	Fantasy of Flight Museum, Polk City, FL	USA
B-17G	44-83559+	*King Bee*	SAC Museum, Lincoln, NE	USA
B-17G	44-83624+	Sleepy Time Gal	AMC Museum, Dover AFB, DL	USA
B-17G	44-83663+	*Short Bier*	Hill AFB Museum, Ogden, UT	USA
B-17G	44-83684+	Picadilly Lily	Planes of Fame Air Museum, Chino, CA	USA
B-17G	44-83690+	*Liberty Belle*	Grissom AFB Museum, Peru, IN	USA
B-17G	44-83718*	MuseuoAerospacial	Rio de Janeiro	Brazil
B-17G	44-83735+	*Mary Alice*	Imperial War Museum, Duxford, Cambs	UK
B-17G	44-83814*	—	National Air and Space Museum, Washington, DC	USA
B-17G	44-83863+	—	USAF Armament Museum, Eglin AFB, Valparaiso, FL	USA
B-17G	44-83868+	—	RAF Museum, Hendon, London	UK
B-17G	44-83884+	*Yankee Doodle Dandy*	8th Air Force Museum, Barksdale AFB, Bossier City, LA	USA
B-17G	44-85583+	—	Base Area de Recife, Recife	Brazil
B-17G	44-85599+	*Reluctant Dragon*	Linear Air Park, Dyess AFB, TX	USA
B-17G	44-85734*	Outhouse Mouse	Randsburg Corp, Kissimmee, FL	USA
B-17G	44-85738+	—	American Veterans Memorial, Tulare, CA	USA
B-17G	44-85790+	Lacey Lady	Lacey's Gas Station, Oregon City, OR	USA
B-17G	44-85828+	*I'll Be Around*	Pima Air and Space Museum, Tucson, AZ	USA

Key: + = On Public Display. ***** = Stored/Under Restoration

Top right: Pictured about to touch down at Duxford, UK, in 1983, B-17G 44-83868 flew the Atlantic to join the Royal Air Force Museum's collection of historic aircraft at Hendon, London, UK. (Key – Duncan Cubitt)

Centre right: Parked on the ramp next to a B-52 Stratofortress, B-17G 44-83559 *King Bee* is preserved at the Strategic Air Command Museum, Lincoln, Nebraska, USA. (Key – Duncan Cubitt)

Bottom right: 44-85599, *The Reluctant Dragon*, an olive drab camouflaged B-17G forms part of the historic aircraft display at the Linear Air Park, Dyess Air Force Base, Texas, USA. (Key – Alan Warnes)

Below: Kermit Weeks' B-17G *Susy Q* is currently undergoing long-term restoration to bring it up to flying condition at his Fantasy of Flight Museum in Florida, USA. (Key – Duncan Cubitt)

Left: 43-38636 *Virgin's Delight* is a B-17G and is currently on show at the Castle Air Force Base Museum, Atwater, California, USA. (Key – Dave Allport)

Top right: Taken from B-17G *Sally B*, this evocative view shows the Royal Air Force Museum's B-17G, 44-83868 (N5237V) on one of its last flights before being grounded and placed inside the display hall at Hendon, London, UK. (Key – Duncan Cubitt)

Centre right: Not part of a military museum, 44-85738, a natural metal B-17G, bears the nose art *Preston Pride* and is kept in fine condition at the American Veteran's Memorial, Tulare, California, USA. (Key – Dave Allport)

Bottom right: *Yankee Doodle Dandy*, the title of the 1942 James Cagney film, adorns the side of B-17G 44-83884, which is on public display at the 8th Air Force Museum, Barksdale Air Force Base, Bossier City, Louisiana, USA. (Key – Alan Warnes)

Bottom left: Many long hours of hard work were expended on the restoration of B-17G 44-83735 *Mary Alice*, which is currently displayed inside the American Air Museum, Duxford, UK. It is considered to be one of the most authentic Flying Fortress survivors. (Key – Steve Fletcher)

Above: B-17G 44-6393 is slowly being put back to static museum configuration at March Field Museum, Riverside, California, USA. As can be seen, work is being carried out in the open. (Key – Dave Allport)

Below: The turretless *Heaven's Above* is a B-17G (44-83512) and has been preserved at the USAF History Museum situated at Lackland Air Force Base, San Antonio, Texas, USA, for many years. (Key – Duncan Cubitt)

Opposite page, top: B-17G 44-83624 *Sleepy Time Gal* was at one time on show at the USAF Museum, Dayton, Ohio, USA, from 1957 to 1988, until the arrival of *Shoo Shoo Shoo Baby*, when it was dismantled and moved to its current home at the AMC Museum, Dover Air Force Base, Delaware. It is pictured in 1971 being towed to the USAF Museum's larger facility, where the bomber could be displayed under cover. (Robert F Dorr)

Opposite page, bottom: B-17G Shoo *Shoo Shoo Baby* is a former 91st Bomb Group aircraft with a confirmed wartime operational history. Due to engine problems it was forced to divert to Sweden, while on a mission to bomb a Focke Wulf Fw 190 factory at Poznan in Poland on May 29, 1944. Interned for the rest of the war, it subsequently flew as a passenger airliner (SE-BAP) and also saw service in this configuration in Denmark (OY-DFA). Between 1947 and 1955 it flew with the France-based Institut Geographique National as F-BGSP and was eventually donated to the USAF Museum by the French government. After being subjected to an eight-year restoration at Dover Air Force Base, Delaware, the bomber flew to its new home at Wright-Patterson AFB, Dayton, Ohio, on October 13, 1988. It remains on display as an excellent representative of the bloody battles fought in the sky over Europe during World War Two. (Robert F Dorr)

8

B-17 VARIANTS AND DEVELOPMENT

Model 299 (XB-17)

Accommodation:	8
Powerplant:	Pratt & Whitney S1EG Hornet radial engines, producing 750hp (559kW) at 2,240 rpm at 7,000ft (2,133m)
Wingspan:	103ft 9 3/8in (31.3m)
Length:	68ft 9in (21.03m)
Height:	14ft 115/16in (4.5m)
Wing Area:	1,420ft2 (131.9m2)
Empty Weight:	21,657lb (9,823kg)
Gross Weight:	32.432lb (14,711kg) (normal), 38,053lb (17,260kg) (maximum)
Max Speed:	236mph (379km/h)
Cruising Speed:	140mph (225km/h) at 70% power
Service Ceiling:	24,620ft (7,504m)
Range:	3,101 miles (4,990km)
Armament:	Five .30 cal machine-guns, eight 600lb (272kg) bombs
C/ns:	1963
Registration:	X-13372

Model 299B (Y1B-17)

Accommodation:	6
Powerplant:	Wright R-1820-39 radial engines, 1,000hp (746kW) (take-off)
Wingspan:	103ft 93/8in (31.3m)
Length:	68ft 4in (20.72m)
Height:	18ft 4in (5.48m)
Wing Area:	1,420ft2 (131.9m2)
Empty Weight:	24,465lb (11,097kg)
Gross Weight:	34,880lb (15,821kg) (normal), 42,600lb (19,323kg) (maximum)
Max Speed:	255mph (410.3km/h)
Cruising Speed:	217mph (349.2km/h)
Service Ceiling:	30,500ft (9,296m)
Range:	1,400 miles (2,253m)
Armament:	Five .30 cal machine-guns, 8,000lb (3,628kg) bombs
C/ns:	1973 – 1985
Army serial numbers:	36-149/161

Model 299M (B-17B)

Accommodation:	6
Powerplant:	Wright R-1820-51 radial engines, 1,200hp (895.2kW) (take off)
Wingspan:	103ft 93/8in (31.69m)
Length:	67ft 9in (20.7m)
Height:	18ft 4in (5.48m)
Wing Area:	1,420ft2 (131.9m2)
Empty Weight:	27,652lb (12,542kg)
Gross Weight:	37,997lb (17,235kg)
Max Speed:	292mph (469km/h)
Cruising Speed:	225mph (362km/h)
Service Ceiling:	30,000ft (9,144m)
Range:	1,250 miles (2,011km)
Armament:	Five .30 cal machine-guns, 8,000lb (3,626kg) bombs
C/ns:	2004 - 2042
Army serial numbers:	38-211/223, 38-258/270, 38-583, 584, 610, 39-1/10

Model 299H (B-17C/D)

Accommodation:	6
Powerplant:	Wright R-1820-65 radial engines, 1,000hp (746kW) at 25,000ft (7,620m)
Wingspan:	103ft 93/8in (31.6m)
Length:	67ft 9in (20.7m)
Height:	18ft 4in (5.48m)
Wing Area:	1,420ft2 (131.9m2)
Empty Weight:	29,021lb (13,163kg)
Gross Weight:	47,242lb (21,428kg)
Max Speed:	323mph (519km/h) at 25,000ft (7,620m)
Range:	2,400 miles (3,862km)
Armament:	Six .30 cal and two .50 cal machine-guns, 4,000lb (1,814kg) bombs
C/ns:	2043 - 2083
Army serial numbers:	40-2042/2079

Right: Just 39 B-17Bs were built, with their delivery to the US Army Air Corps starting in October 1938. Remarkably the final B-17B variant was not retired until 1946. (Robert F Dorr)

Centre right: Wearing the incorrect serial AM528 (it should be AN528), this aircraft was one of 20 B-17Cs operated by the Royal Air Force as Fortress Is. Proving to be unsuitable for the tasks allocated to them by the RAF, the Fortresses went on to serve with Coastal Command. (Key Collection)

Bottom right: The American counterpart to the RAF's Fortress I, 28-2B, a B-17C, flew with the 2nd Bomb Group in late 1941. (Pete West)

Below: A Boeing YB-17 taxis out wearing the tail code BB 50. Note the intakes for the engine superchargers mounted on top of the nacelles, a feature that was missing from the previous Y1B-17A model. (Robert F Dorr)

Model 299 O (B-17F)

Accommodation:	10
Powerplant:	Wright R-1820-97 radial engines, 1,200hp (895.2kW) at 25,000ft (7,620m)
Wingspan:	103ft 9in (31.6m)
Length:	74ft 9in (22.8m)
Height:	19ft 2in (5.79m)
Wing Area:	1,420ft2 (131.9m2)
Empty Weight:	34,000lb (15,422kg)
Gross Weight:	56,500lb (25,628kg)
Max Speed:	299mph (481km/h) at 25,000ft (7,620m)
Cruising Speed:	160mph (257km/h) at 5,000ft (1,524m)
Service Ceiling:	37,500ft (11,430m)
Range:	1,300 miles (2,092km) with 6,000lb (2,721kg) bombs
Armament:	Ten .50 cal machine-guns, 6,000lb (2,721kg) bombs
C/ns:	Boeing: 3025 - 3324, 3589 - 4023, 4581 - 6145; Douglas: 7900 - 8501, 8503 - 8506; Lockheed Vega: 6001 - 6500
Army serial numbers:	Boeing: 41-24340/24639, 42-5050/5484, 42-29467/31031; Douglas: 42-2964/3562, 42-33714/33715, 42-33717/37220; Lockheed Vega: 42-5705/6204

Model 299 O (B-17E)

Accommodation:	6-10
Powerplant:	Wright R-1820-65 radial engines, 1,200hp (895.2kW) at 25,000ft (7,620m)
Wingspan:	103ft 9in (31.6m)
Length:	73ft 10in (22.5m)
Height:	19ft 2in (5.79m)
Wing Area:	1,420ft2 (131.9m2)
Empty Weight:	33,279lb (15,095kg)
Gross Weight:	53,000lb (24,040kg)
Max Speed:	317mph (510.1km/h) at 25,000ft (7,620m)
Cruising Speed:	224mph (360km/h) at 15,000ft (4,572m)
Service Ceiling:	36,600ft (11,155m)
Range:	2,000 miles (3,218m) with 4,000lb (1,814kg) bombs
Armament:	One .30 cal and eight .50 cal machine-guns, 4,000lb (1,814kg) bombs
C/ns:	2204 - 2480, 2483 - 2717
Army serial numbers:	41-2393/2669, 41-9011/9245

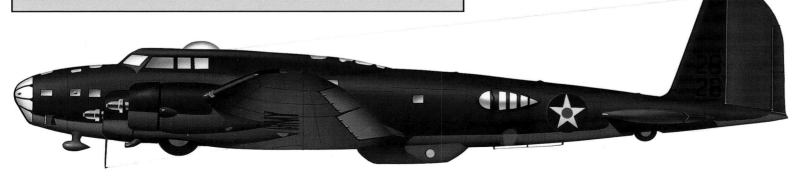

Left: This early publicity photograph depicts Boeing B-17E 41-2656 during a test flight. The legends *Chief Seattle* and *From The Pacific Northwest* appear on the nose, possibly making this the first use of nicknames on a B-17. The early-style national insignia was changed fairly rapidly in order to stem any confusion with the Japanese national 'meatball' emblem. This particular bomber was one of a group which saw service with the 9th Bomb Squadron, 7th Bomb Group and was based on the island of Java in early 1942. (Robert F Dorr)

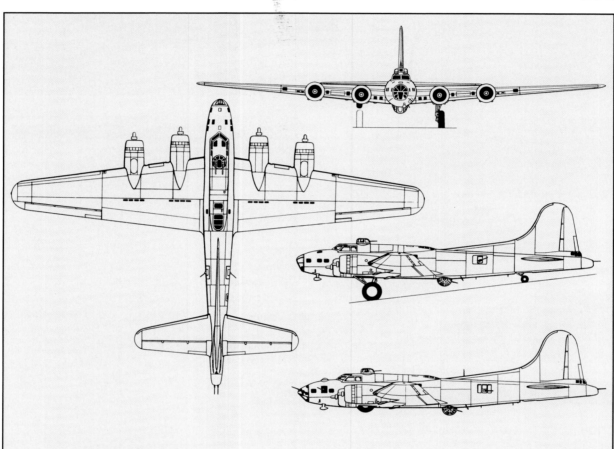

Left: The basic differences in the nose areas of the B-17E and B-17F are illustrated in these three view drawings. The plan view is that of a B-17E. (Key Collection)

Below: *Lakanuki* and *Oh Nausea!*, a pair of B-17Fs receive final maintenance before departing for a mission in the Pacific theatre of operations. (Robert F Dorr)

Top: The quintessential natural metal B-17G – as many of the marque appeared in the latter years of World War Two. This aircraft, which has yet to be allocated to an operational unit, and is believed to be pictured on a test flight, as it has its waist gun positions blanked off. (US National Archives)

Above: WB-17G 44-85795 of an unknown unit, carrying the nose legend *Weather Radar Research*, photographed at Logon Airport, Massachusetts, USA, on May 16, 1948. (Robert F Dorr)

Model 299-0 (B-17G)		Construction numbers:	Boeing: 6146 - 7230, 7531 - 7880, 7881 - 8480, 8487 - 10486; Douglas: 8419 - 8499, 8500 - 8999, 21899 - 22148, 22224 - 23223, 31877 - 32526; Lockheed Vega: 6501 - 6800, 6801 - 7400, 7401 - 8400, 8401 - 8750
Accommodation:	10		
Powerplant:	Wright R-1820-97 radial engines, 1,200hp (985.2kW) at 25,000ft (7,620m)		
Wingspan:	103ft 9in (31.6m)		
Length:	74ft 9in (22.8m)		
Height:	19ft 2in (5.79m)		
Wing Area:	1,420ft2 (131.9m2)	**Army serial numbers:**	Boeing: 42-31032/32116, 42- 97058/97407, 42- 102379/102978, 43- 37509/39608; Douglas: 42- 3483/3563, 42- 37714/38213, 42-106984/107233, 44- 6001/7000, 44- 83236/83885; Lockheed Vega: 42- 39758/40057, 42-97436/98035, 44-8110/9000, 44- 85492/85841
Empty Weight:	36,135lb (16,390kg)		
Gross Weight:	65,500lb (29,710kg)		
Max Speed:	287mph (461km/h) at 25,000ft (7,620m)		
Cruising Speed:	150mph (241km/h) at 5,000ft (1,524m)		
Service Ceiling:	35,600ft (10,850m)		
Range:	2,000 miles (3,218km) with 6,000lb (2,721kg) bombs		
Armament:	11-13 .50 cal machine-guns, 9,600lb (4,354kg) bombs		

All subsequent designations, up to B-17P, were airframe conversions, eg B-17H and TB-17H were search and rescue aircraft, which were equipped to carry airborne lifeboats that were dropped at sea, by means of three parachutes.

Top left: Boeing MB-17G 43-39119 was assigned to the Eglin Field Test Centre, Florida, in March 1945 to test JB-2 *Loon* missiles. JB-2s were former German V-1 flying bombs of the type used against the UK during the latter part of World War Two. (Robert F Dorr)

Left: Close-up view of the 'doodlebug' installation on the MB-17. As can be seen, ground clearance was minimal. Note the US national insignia on the fuselage of the *Loon*. (Robert F Dorr)

Left: Present at the Boeing factory at Washington on June 30, 1956, as part of a display to show the different Boeing bombers still in service, VB-17G 43-39356 was assigned to the 8th Air Division. (Robert F Dorr)

Below left: The SB-17G was one of the most visually different of all the Flying Fortress variants. This specialised B-17 was used for dropping lifeboats to downed airmen. Initial development began in 1943 but delays in obtaining suitable airframes meant that this variant did not actually enter service until March 1945. Fitted with a 27ft (8.2m) Higgins A-1 lifeboat, the B-17 had its defensive armament deleted to save weight, and normally operated with an H2X radar radome in place of the chin turret. (Key Collection)

Right: Variations on a theme.

1 Boeing XC-108 (B-17E 41-2593 converted to personal transport for General Douglas MacArthur by deleting armour and some armament and installing extra windows, office, living and cooking accommodation).

2 XB-38 (B-17E 41-2401 with Allison in-line engines).

3 XB-40 (Boeing-built B-17F 41-24341, converted by Vega with additional firepower as an experimental bomber escort).

4 F-9C (one of ten B-17Gs converted to photo-reconnaissance configuration.

5 Re-designated in 1948 to RB-17G) and PB-1W (one of 31 B-17Gs used by the US Navy for anti-submarine warfare, for which a large radome accommodating search radar, was attached to the fuselage underside). (Key Collection)

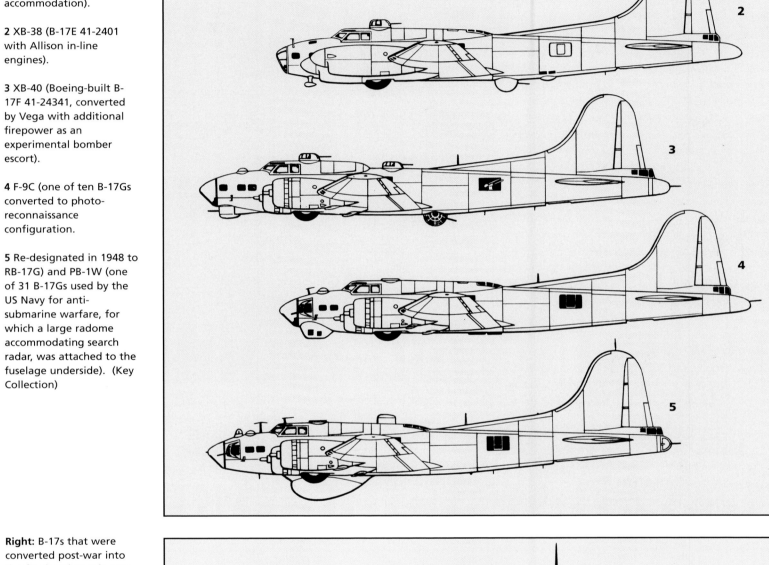

Right: B-17s that were converted post-war into the fire bomber role saw the airframes being stripped of all armament and armour and the installation of large retardant tanks in the bomb bay. (Key Collection)

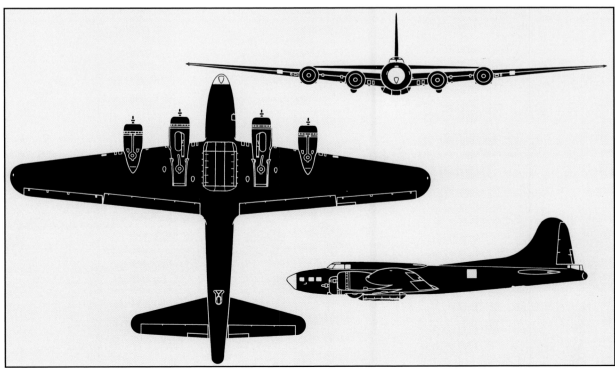

IN 1989 the impressive sight of five Boeing B-17 Flying Fortresses, five Mustangs, three Messerschmitt Bf 109s (albeit Spanish-built), and a B-25 Mitchell camera ship could be seen at the Imperial War Museum's Duxford Airfield, Cambridgeshire, UK. This imposing cadre of vintage aircraft had been gathered together to film sequences for the Warner Brothers/Enigma Films production of *Memphis Belle*. This equalled the number of B-17s that had been gathered together for a film since *Tora, Tora, Tora* back in 1970. Then a total of five were mustered (N17W, N620L, N621L, N3193 and N9563Z), of which one would re-appear in front of the cameras again for *Memphis Belle*.

The plan to remake William Wyler's famous wartime documentary/propaganda film came from his daughter, Catherine Wyler, who with David Puttnam, then head of Columbia Pictures in the USA, first mooted the idea in 1986. This original scheme did not proceed very far as Puttnam left his post at Columbia and returned to the UK in order to re-launch his previous company, Enigma Films. However, the idea did not die, as Catherine Wyler soon joined Puttnam as co-producer for the venture. After initially being titled *Memphis Belle*, it was re-named *Southern Belle* so as not to be labelled a straight remake of the wartime film. As research progressed into the subject it was discovered that at least three wartime Flying Fortresses had the name *Southern Belle*, so the studios, aware of the legal implications on using this title, quickly reverted the film back to *Memphis Belle*.

It was originally thought that all filming could be conducted in the USA, where there was a plentiful supply of airworthy B-17s. Difficulties were then experienced in finding a suitable airfield location that could double for wartime England. It is also reported that problems had occurred in agreeing suitable fees for the owners of certain B-17s.

Puttnam and Wyler's attentions then turned to Europe. It transpired that three B-17s were available in France and Britain, and negotiations were started with a pair of Flying Fortress operators in the USA to see if they could be persuaded to fly their aircraft across the Atlantic to join in the filming. Fees were worked out and Bob Richardson, owner of B-17F 42-29782 (N17W), and David Tallichet, operator of B-17G 44-83546 (N3703G) were contracted to provide their aircraft. Meanwhile the UK-based B-17G

One of the most realistic documentary films to emanate from World War Two was, undoubtedly, *Memphis Belle*. Telling the story of a B-17, and its crew, which survived 25 missions in the European Theatre of Operations was not going to be an easy task for the USAAF's Army Pictorial Service. Famed Hollywood producer/director William Wyler was given the task of putting this charismatic tale onto the silver screen.

Early on in the process a decision was taken to shoot the film using 16mm colour film in order to give it more impact at a period when most films were made using monochrome stock.

Wyler assembled a specialised team of cameramen, all of whom had to acquire the necessary aerial gunnery and aircraft recognition skills in a two-week course at Bovingdon, Herts, UK, before a single foot of film passed through the cameras. It was decided to concentrate on the operations of the 8th Air Force's 91st Bomb Group, based at Bassingbourn, which had good road communications with Wyler's base in London.

Filming during real combat conditions was not easy, the cameras in use only had a capacity of just over two minutes of film, before the reel had to be changed, subjecting the cameramen, who had to remove their gloves to carry out this task, to the risks of frostbite at the high altitudes flown by the B-17s.

As filming progressed the storyline was developed around a B-17F, *Memphis Belle*, which was approaching the hallowed 25-mission status. In the event the *Memphis Belle* was not the first to complete 25 missions, but for dramatic purposes it was implied that the bomber was the first to reach this total in the UK. Under the captaincy of Robert Morgan the mission total was attained on May 17, 1943, and William Wyler arranged for the bomber to be flown back to the USA where it would prove to be an invaluable tool for publicising the finished film.

With a running time of 38 minutes, narration by Lester Koenig and music by Gail Kubik, *Memphis Belle* stands as one of World War Two's film icons. It was released onto the cinema circuits on April 15, 1944, and is the film by which all other wartime documentaries have subsequently been measured.

44-85784 (G-BEDF) *Sally B*, and the two French machines, B-17G 44-8846 (F-AZDX) operated by Association Fortresse Toujours Volant en France, and B-17G 44-85643 (F-BEEA) the final example flown by the Institut Geographique National (IGN) were being readied for their bouts of cinematic stardom.

Enigma Film's art department faced the large task of making all of the bombers resemble the early B-17F variant. Little work had to be carried out on Bob Richardson's aircraft, as it was the correct mark already, but various changes had to be made to the remainder of

Top right: David Tallichet's B-17G is 'made up' to resemble the *Memphis Belle* at Duxford during the summer of 1989. The bomber's somewhat weathered appearance was concocted by the film's art department and was effective in portraying a well used aircraft. (Key – Duncan Cubitt)

Bottom right: Executing a steep pull up after a run and break at Duxford, the sun glints off the wing of one of the Fortresses. (Key – Duncan Cubitt)

Left: Some close-up taxying shots of the French-based F-AZDX *Mother and Country* were filmed at Duxford, whereas the main ground filming took place at Binbrook in Lincolnshire. (Key – Duncan Cubitt)

FILM APPEARANCES BY B-17 FLYING FORTRESSES			
Test Pilot 1938	The Memphis Belle..............1944	Command Decision.............1948	Top of the World................1955
I Wanted Wings 1941	Passage to Marseilles 1944	Task Force 1949	Lady Takes a Flier 1957
Flying Fortress 1941	Hotel Berlin 1945	Twelve O'Clock High 1949	The War Lover.....................1961
Air Force 1943	Sunday Dinner for	When Willie Comes	Thunderball.........................1965
Bombardier 1943	Soldier Fox........................1945	Marching home 1950	The Biggest Bundle of
Aerial Gunner 1943	Captain Eddie 1945	Chain Lightning 1950	Them All 1968
Hers to Hold 1943	You Came Along.................1945	Above and Beyond..............1952	Thousand Plane Raid..........1969
The Sky's the Limit 1943	Best Years of Our Lives........1946	Operation Secret 1952	Tora, Tora, Tora 1970
Ladies Courageous..............1944	Fighter Squadron 1948	The High and the Mighty 1954	Memphis Belle 1990

Far left: The 'acting' crew of *Memphis Belle* pose for a publicity shot alongside David Tallichet's 44-83546 (N3703G) during the filming at Binbrook. (Warner Bros)

Left: As with any aviation filmwork, the aircraft involved wore a number of different sets of markings and nose art. *Mother and Country*, representing a new aircraft on the squadron, hence no weathering, is the French-based F-AZDX, while *Baby Ruth*, in the background, is the ill-fated IGN aircraft, F-BEEA. (Key – Duncan Cubitt)

Far left: Atmospheric shot of B-17s at Binbrook during the early morning light as the groundcrews prepare their charges for battle. (Warner Bros)

Left: The film's art department was responsible for the fake weathering applied to all the aircraft used in the movie. Faded camouflage, scratches and oil stains were all created by the skills of the cinema backroom boys. (Key – Duncan Cubitt)

Left: On the whole, aircraft serviceability was fairly good throughout the filming schedule, although F-AZDX had to undergo a powerplant change after blowing a cylinder from its No 1 engine during a filming sortie. (Robert J Rudhall)

Right: The UK-based *Sally B* was the only Fortress which was fitted with smoke ejectors for the movie and is pictured here post-filming at the 1989 Great Warbirds Air Display wearing 'DF-Z' codes. (Key – Duncan Cubitt)

the 'cast'. Upper gun turrets, ball turrets and tail turrets, plus guns, all had to be modified. Alterations also had to be made to waist gun windows in order to configure them in the correct style for the period.

With all five Fortresses gathered together, they were repainted into uniform period markings at Southend Airport, Essex. Apart from the bombers the film-makers had also managed to get together five Mustang fighters to act as bomber escorts. As happens so often in the film world, artistic licence came into play, and five late war-style P-51D Mustangs (G-BIXL, G-HAEC, G-SUSY, N167F and N51JJ) were hired and painted in earlier P-51B camouflage and markings. Three Spanish-built Messerschmitt 109s (G-BOML, G-HHUN and D-FEHD), seen together on screen during the previous year in the television series *Piece of Cake*, portrayed the role of the enemy. This constituted the largest number of vintage aircraft used for filmwork at Duxford Airfield since the making of the United Artists film *Battle of Britain* in 1968.

After a frenzy of activity, filming finally got underway in late June with all aircraft based at the Cambridgeshire air museum, along with the cameraship, Aces High's B-25J Mitchell N1042B, a veteran of many filming sorties. Visitors to Duxford during this period were treated to some incredible sights as all of the aircraft got airborne and set off for the filming sorties. By mid-July all of the aerial shots were 'in the can' and the company moved out to its 'airfield location' for the ground scenes.

Binbrook in Lincolnshire, a former RAF Lightning jet fighter base, had been taken over by Enigma Films and for several weeks previous to the aircraft arriving work was carried out to turn the modern military airfield into a wartime bomber base. Temporary buildings had been erected, dummy Flying Fortresses had been built, many of

which were just one dimensional 'flats', which would only be seen in 'long shot'.

On the whole filming progressed well on the ground-bound and take off sequences for the film. However, tragedy struck on July 25 when, during a take off sequence, the IGN-operated Fortress 44-85643 (F-BEEA) encountered a serious problem, which saw the bomber leaving the runway and crashing into a field. Although all ten people on board the aircraft got out fairly unscathed, the bomber caught fire and was totally burnt out.

By early August the bulk of the filming was completed and the aircraft started to disperse to their home bases. Like most feature films that have been centred around aircraft, *Memphis Belle* was not a roaring success at the box office. However, its business was reasonable and in terms of its authenticity, the makers scored highly in their efforts to get the wartime details as correct as they could. The casting of relatively unknown actors to take the lead roles (Matthew Modine, Eric Stoltz, Billy Zane, Harry Connick Jr etc) was a stroke of genius as it made the whole story more believable, instead of the usual 'movie star playing the pilot' scenario so often employed by film companies.

Considering the advancement of the film industry's special effects departments during the 1970s and 1980s, it has to be said that some of the model work in *Memphis Belle* was distinctly suspect and unconvincing. That apart, to get five Flying Fortresses, five Mustangs and three Messerschmitts together in England during 1989 was a very laudable achievement, and one which may never be repeated. Two of the bombers which appeared in *Memphis Belle* still retain their film markings, David Tallichet's B-17G *Memphis Belle* 44-83546 (N3703G) and B-17 Preservation's B-17G *Sally B*, 44-85784 (G-BEDF) and as such act as a reminder of the Flying Fortresses last (so far) starring role on the cinema screen.

During the latter years of World War Two, many say that the UK resembled a huge aircraft carrier, with airfields liberally dotted around the countryside. Land was requisitioned from its owners, many of them farmers, and airfields sprang up, seemingly overnight! The building programmes, not only for the airfields themselves, but also for the associated infrastructure and accommodation, were extensive to say the least – whole communities were created. At the end of hostilities, some of these developments disappeared almost as fast as they had appeared. Others still survive as active flying sites, but the majority have reverted to their previous use and bear little evidence of their wartime heritage.

Note: Many UK county boundaries have changed since the end of World War Two – airfields may then have come under a different county authority; we have listed their present location.

Top left: Initially constructed as a satellite airfield for RAF Wyton, Alconbury, Cambs, accommodated the 93rd Bomb Group, which became known as the 'Travelling Circus'. The airfield covered some 500 acres, of which 100 acres comprised concrete hardstandings for the aircraft. Later, the 92nd Bomb Group, 'Fame's Favoured Few', moved in, as did the 482nd Bomb Group, the latter being the only Group to be officially activated in the UK. Post-war Alconbury was kept busy with USAF F-4 Phantoms and A-10 Thunderbolt IIs until its closure in the early 1990s. It is no longer an active airfield and was subsequently earmarked for development. (Key – Ken Delve)

Centre left: Glatton, Cambs, sometimes known as Conington, was home to B-17s of the 457th Bomb Group – the final Fortress Group to be assigned to the 1st Air Division. Glatton was unique in that its runways enclosed a working farm, which carried on regardless of the vast influx of men and machines. Over 2,900 personnel were dispersed in living accommodation within the surrounding countryside. During the post-war modernisation of the nearby A1 trunk road, much of the hardcore was obtained from Glatton's runways and hardstandings, although the wartime layout of the airfield can still be seen. Aviation activity continues here as the site is used for business and light aviation, serving the nearby city of Peterborough. (Key – Ken Delve)

Bottom left: With the familiar triangle of runways still visible, Grafton Underwood, Northants, is one of those locations where memories of the US 8th Air Force linger on. It was built to the then standard wartime pattern to provide a hard-surfaced bomber station for the RAF's 8 Group. But it had to be enlarged to accommodate American bombers and ended up with 50 hardstandings, plus a pair of T.2 hangars. After being used by Douglas Bostons, it received two squadrons of B-17Es in July 1942, when the 97th Bomb Group used it as a satellite airfield for Polebrook, Northants. In September, two elements of the 305th Bomb Group arrived and operations started the following month. Later, the 384th Bomb Group took up residence, remaining until the end of the war. It closed in 1959, and the airfield reverted to its previous use. In 1977 a memorial to the 384th BG was erected – the Duxford-based B-17G *Sally B* flying over in tribute during the unveiling ceremony. (Key – Ken Delve)

Above: As 15 Flying Fortresses pass overhead, a solitary B-17 from the 379th Bomb Group sits on the ground at Kimbolton, the USAAF's Station 117. (US National Archives)

Top right: Originally built to house RAF bombers, by September 1942 Kimbolton, Cambs, was occupied by B-17s of the 91st Bomb Group. This unit moved on to Bassingbourn, Cambs, after only one month at Kimbolton, and was replaced by the 379th, the most successful of all the 8th Air Force bomber groups. General James Doolittle (of attack on Tokyo fame) paid a visit on March 6, 1944, and certainly had luck on his side when a returning B-17 got into difficulties and only just cleared the control tower on which he was standing. Post-war, part of the airfield was sold to the Duke of Manchester and it later became an industrial estate. Evidence of its wartime use can still be seen from the air (Key – Ken Delve)

Below: Now known as Santa Pod and synonymous with drag car racing, Podington, Beds, was originally constructed to house two RAF bomber squadrons. In 1942 it was made available to the US 8th Air Force and was first inhabited by the Douglas Boston-equipped 15th Bomb Squadron. This unit gave way to the B-17s of the 100th Bomb Group, although its tenure was short. The 92nd Bomb Group, having left Alconbury, moved in during September 1943. When this unit left Podington in July 1945, the airfield reverted to RAF jurisdiction and was used for storage. During the mid-1960s the main runway was converted for use as a drag strip, and where B-17s once thundered off to fight the enemy, drag cars now burn rubber to reach the finish line. (Key – Ken Delve)
Inset: Construction work can be seen taking place in the vicinity of Podington's control tower. (US National Archives)

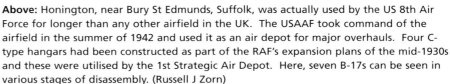

Above: Honington, near Bury St Edmunds, Suffolk, was actually used by the US 8th Air Force for longer than any other airfield in the UK. The USAAF took command of the airfield in the summer of 1942 and used it as an air depot for major overhauls. Four C-type hangars had been constructed as part of the RAF's expansion plans of the mid-1930s and these were utilised by the 1st Strategic Air Depot. Here, seven B-17s can be seen in various stages of disassembly. (Russell J Zorn)

Left: Built as a permanent RAF station in the late 1930s, Watton, Norfolk, was taken over by the USAAF in 1943 to accommodate the 3rd Strategic Air Depot, which repaired and overhauled B-24 Liberators. The 802nd Reconnaissance Group also occupied the site at the same time. In August 1944 three weather squadrons were formed, one of which used B-17s and B-24s for long-range weather observation duties. British-built de Havilland Mosquito aircraft, operated by the USAAF, were also used for photographic and weather patrols in combat areas. When the American units left Watton in mid-1945, the site returned to the control of the RAF. The airfield, although substantially intact, is no longer used for flying purposes. (Key – Ken Delve)

Below: Officers and some of the 'top brass' gather on the control tower at Molesworth, Cambs, waiting for based aircraft of the 303rd Bomb Group to return from a raid. 44-8328, a 'BN'-coded B-17G, is parked alongside one of the T.2 hangars. (US National Archives)

Left: Four of the wartime hangars remain, but little else can be seen of Molesworth's wartime history in this aerial view, taken in 2000. It is still used as one of the USAF's Strategic Operations Centres. (Key – Ken Delve)

Above: B-17s as far as the eye can see! Fortresses of the 381st Bomb Group taxi out to the main runway at Ridgewell, Essex, for the start of another mission. (US National Archives)

Left: 'Somewhere in England'. A B-17G of the 398th Bomb Group is seen running up its engines at Nuthampstead, Herts. (US National Archives)

Right: Chelveston, Northants, seen here in November 2000, was handed over to the USAAF in 1942. Initially home to B-17Fs of the 301st Bomb Group, the unit was replaced by the 305th when it transferred from Grafton Underwood. The 305th led the infamous raid on Schweinfurt, Germany, on October 14, 1944, during which heavy losses were sustained. Reverting to RAF jurisdiction in October 1945, Chelveston moved back into USAF hands in December 1952, when it was used as a readiness station to receive units from the USA should an emergency arise. It has since returned to farmland, but the outlines of the runways can still be seen from the air. (Key – Ken Delve)

Above: A snowy scene at Deenethorpe, Northants, in the winter of 1943/1944. Groundcrews often had to cope with harsh conditions as much of the major work on aircraft was undertaken in the open. The airfield was occupied by B-17Gs of the 401st in November 1943, and operations began later that same month. After flying over 250 missions, the unit returned to the USA in July 1945, its task complete. (Key Collection)

Right: Bedford – or Thurleigh, Beds, as it was known during World War Two – played host to the 306th Bomb Group's B-17Gs from mid-1944. It's now a shadow of its former self, and is used for vehicle storage. Having arrived in September 1942, the 306th remained until December 1945 – marking up the longest tenure of a UK airfield by an American combat unit. It was also in continuous combat use longer than any other, the 306th flying over 340 missions from this site. Post-war it became the home of the Royal Aircraft Establishment, which carried out experimental work for the Ministry of Defence. The RAE relocated to Farnborough and flying ceased at Bedford on March 31, 1994. (Key – Ken Delve)

Bottom right: Sadly no long line of B-17s can be seen at Ridgewell today. The few remaining wartime buildings are accompanied by modern-day glider trailers. Where once the sound of Wright Cyclones filled the sky, only the swish of glider wings can now be heard. (Key – Ken Delve)

Above: While this photo-study has concentrated on the UK airfields, Fortresses flew from many other countries during World War Two. This unusually camouflaged B-17E (12426) is seen at the 13th Air Depot's airfield at Tontouta, New Guinea. The bomber is accompanied by a pair of Martin B-26 Marauders, plus a Lockheed P-38 Lightning and Bell P-39 Airacobra. (US National Archives)

Top left: After operating Consolidated B-24 Liberators, the 487th Bomb Group, based at Lavenham (seen here in 2002) converted to B-17G Flying Fortresses. The unit was initially commanded by Lt Col Beirne Lay Jr, who wrote the screenplay for the famous 1949 film *Twelve O' Clock High*. (Key – Ken Delve)

Top right: Earls Colne, Essex, was home to the 94th Bomb Group for just one month during 1943. It was from here that the 94th carried out its first operational mission, an attack on Antwerp, using 21 B-17s. The airfield is now a shadow of its wartime self and is used by light aircraft. The adjacent golf course, part of the current leisure and country club's facilities, can be seen taking up a large chunk of the World War Two site in this 2002 view. (Key – Ken Delve)

Middle left: Perhaps the most well known of all the Flying Fortress fields in the UK, Bassingbourn was the home of the famous B-17F *Memphis Belle*. Post war English Electric Canberra jet bombers were based with the RAF and the airfield, or what's left of it, is now occupied by the Army. (Key – Ken Delve)

Middle right: Now used as a racing track and weekend market venue, Snetterton Heath was home to the 96th Bomb Group, 8th AF from May 1943 until May 1945. The B-17s of this group led the first shuttle mission, Regensburg – Africa, on August 17, 1943. (Key – Ken Delve)

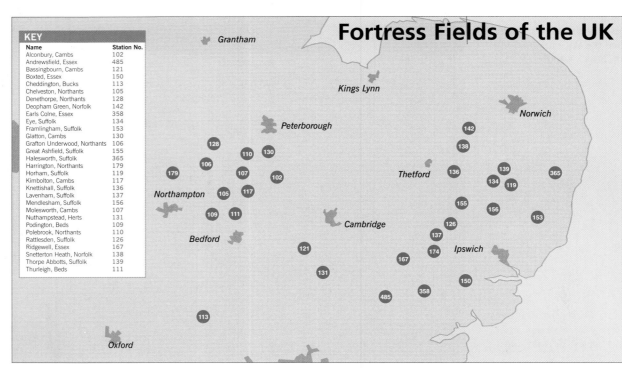

Fortress Fields of the UK

KEY	
Name	**Station No.**
Alconbury, Cambs	102
Andrewsfield, Essex	485
Bassingbourn, Cambs	121
Boxted, Essex	150
Cheddington, Bucks	113
Chelveston, Northants	105
Denethorpe, Northants	128
Deopham Green, Norfolk	142
Earls Colne, Essex	358
Eye, Suffolk	134
Framlingham, Suffolk	153
Glatton, Cambs	130
Grafton Underwood, Northants	106
Great Ashfield, Suffolk	155
Halesworth, Suffolk	365
Harrington, Northants	179
Horham, Suffolk	119
Kimbolton, Cambs	117
Knettishall, Suffolk	136
Lavenham, Suffolk	137
Mendlesham, Suffolk	156
Molesworth, Cambs	107
Nuthampstead, Herts	131
Podington, Beds	109
Polebrook, Northants	110
Rattlesden, Suffolk	126
Ridgewell, Essex	167
Snetterton Heath, Norfolk	138
Thorpe Abbotts, Suffolk	139
Thurleigh, Beds	111

Below: B-17G *Sally B* flies over a 'patchwork quilt' of British countryside. These 'fields' supported many USAAF airbases during the dark days of World War Two. (Key – Duncan Cubitt)

Overleaf: B-17 Flying Fortress – a living legend. (Key – Duncan Cubitt)